THE PAINTINGS OF
ART PINAJIAN

A Family Story

Pete and Archie, circa 1987

THE PAINTINGS OF ART PINAJIAN

A Family Story

Pete Najarian

REGENT PRESS
Berkeley, California

{paperback}
ISBN 13: 978-1-58790-321-2
ISBN 10: 1-58790-321-0

{e-book}
ISBN 13: 978-1-58790-324-3
ISBN 10: 1-58790-324-5

Library of Congress Control Number: 2015940382

Cover Illustration: oil on canvas, 1989

Printed in the U.S.A.

REGENT PRESS
Berkeley, California
www.regentpress.net

This book is for my dear old friend,
Bobby Ohannesian,
and for all my other friends
who have also been so kind to me.

It is a sequel to *The Artist and His Mother.*

*Bobby, watching T.V. and lying on his couch with his head
on a pillow, 1984. In pencil, by Pete, first learning how to draw.*

Art and Death

If *this were a movie* it would begin in a little dump by the railroad tracks at the edge of a small New Jersey suburb called Tenafly, across the river from Manhattan near the George Washington Bridge.

Then the camera moves to an artist, who in real life was my cousin Charlie, coming by one morning, let's say in the 1950's, though it could have been a decade later, and the manager of the dump says to him:

"Hey, Charlie, I have another frame for you."

And so we know he would save old paintings for Charlie who would buy their frames before the canvasses were dumped into the rest of the landfill.

But on this morning it is the canvas that catches Charlie's eye, a first-rate landscape by an academic artist whose name I had forgotten until I just recovered it, thanks to Google and what Charlie once told me.

There happened to live in Tenafly another artist, Harvey Dunn, 1884-1952, who must have exchanged work with a friend, as artist friends often do, and Dunn's survivors, who lived near Charlie, must have dumped the friend's landscape after Dunn had died.

And for whatever reason my old memory remembers some names and forgets others, the name Dunn stayed with me; so when I Googled him and learned that he shared a school in the nearby town of Leonia with a George Chapman, I Googled Chapman and saw that, yes, his work was like the landscape Charlie had found in the Tenafly dump.

If you Google Charlie now, Charles Mazoujian, 1917-2011, you will see only the cover of a comic book he illustrated in 1939, and the cover of a book about the U.S. Marines in 1951. But if you look further you may learn that his best works are the watercolors he painted in the Forties, one of which won a national prize.

After he had moved to an assisted living home near his daughter Gwen, she shipped what remained of his work to a storage near her home in Sacramento; but when I called her about the Chapman painting she said it was gone and the movers must have stolen it after Charlie spilled the beans about how valuable it was.

And so returning now to my movie about salvaged and stolen paintings, let's flash forward to another dump, or rather the dump truck in which I once dumped a pile of my cousin Archie's paintings after he too had died.

If you Google Archie now, Art Pinajian, 1914-1999, you will find what the promoter of his work has published about him, much of it from my own unpublished biography that I'm now revising after the promoter's distortions and errors.

There was however nothing about Archie on Google at the time of his death, since he had become very isolated by then, especially after he and his sister Armen had moved to an out of the way little town called Bellport on the south shore of Long Island.

I was by then the only one left who could deal with his work, since Armen was incapable of such an enormous task, and even I had been dreading it after I had asked him on one of my visits back east:

"What are you going to do with all this work, Archie?"

And he said what I had feared since I had first fallen in love with him:

"I'm leaving it all to you."

You can imagine now what this meant to me if I say to any of you that I'm leaving you all my work after I die.

None of you of course will hop on the first plane you can find and get here before it all gets dumped, but that's exactly what I had to do when Armen called while I was caring for my mother who had just broken her hip, and my brother shouted at me from where he was vacationing:

"You care more about more about Archie than you do your own mother!"

I didn't of course, but I still had to tell him that he had to rush back to Mama because I had to rush to Bellport before the start of my new class, since this would be the only time I'd have free.

It would turn out, however, here now sixteen years after all those paintings were virtually stolen from me, that had I stayed with my mother and never gone back it would have made no difference.

Yet that morning when Armen was crying over the phone, I was not only filled with shock and grief, but a terrible panic at what I had been dreading, and since you all know of my dreadful personality you can imagine what a state I was in.

And so I flew back on the first flight I could find, and for the next two weeks I struggled like Hercules in the Augean Stables to salvage whatever I could of my beloved Archie's work, and a huge stack of it had become so moldy in the dirt floor garage that I had to pile it on the street for the garbage truck.

And when the garbage men began to haul away his old paint cans and leftovers that I had to dig through like you would have to dig here after I'm gone, I asked them to please let me dump the moldy paintings myself, as if they were somehow sacred and not to be touched by an unbeliever.

Then carrying them in my arms like a dead body on a battlefield, I dumped them into the black hole of the truck that had become the very black hole of the universe that would swallow not only his life's work but that of every artist from all the way back to the caves and even the great pyramids in the desert sands that are supposed to be eternal.

And this is how my movie would end, with the dump truck driving away and the camera of my memory watching it disappear around the corner, not knowing that what I had struggled so hard to save would disappear for me as well, just like the Chapman painting Charlie had saved that is now who knows where in some Antique Roadshow or thrift shop.

* * *

In the meantime, back in 1951, when I was turning eleven and Harvey Dunn was about to die, my mother and I and Archie and Armen took the bus one Sunday to Charlie's new home in Tenafly, which seemed like another country in those days when the rest of us were still living in the crowded tenements of West Hoboken.

It was by today's standards a modest home, yet compared to the little railroad rooms where I lived with my mother, it was like a dream house with a big window looking out to the woods, and there was even a stream running wild as if in a western movie.

I hardly knew Charlie at the time, in fact I can't remember him before then, and yet I felt close to him not only from the photos of our family album, but the watercolor he had given my mother before he was drafted, which would become one of the most important icons of my life.

He had been drafted in the year I was born, 1940, and so he was gone all during the war; and afterwards he and Edna lived with her parents in Brooklyn while he taught at Pratt Art Institute and worked free-lance until he could afford the down payment on the Tenafly house.

He had painted the watercolor when he was only eighteen, and when he happened to see it again in his old age he would notice only "the mistakes in it." Yet I would treasure it as much as a Rembrandt or a Da Vinci, since I had been looking at it from when I first opened my eyes.

There are many watercolors as good and even better all over the world, but it was special to me because it was my first window

Charlie's watercolor at age 18 [Color altered by reproduction.]

into the world of art that I would be longing to enter for the rest
of my life.

"When Charlie was a kid," Archie once told me, "he could
draw as well as Sargent," and Sargent in fact had been Charlie's
hero; but there is more to art than talent, and what would happen
to Charlie's will be part of the story I'm about to tell you.

Archie too had the same talent, but by 1951 he had taken a
different road from the one he had shared with Charlie when they
were kids like me, and standing with them together for the first
time in Charlie's new home, I imagined myself like the boy in the
attached photo of my father standing with his two older brothers
in a golden age before it was turned into hell by the massacre.

Forgive me now for squeezing so many figures and scenes here
all at once, but I need to introduce my main theme right away,
which will be about the interface of art and what we call history
and death.

My father was born in the ancient city of Tigranakert that is
now called Diyarbekir in eastern Turkey, and since he was born in
1893, the photo of him must
have been about ten years later,
before his brothers, who were
leaders of an underground resistance group, were executed
during the Armenian genocide.

The figure holding his
tool is Boghos, who was an
architect, and next to him is
Garabed, who was a build-
er, and my father Armenag is
standing at their side.

Boghos and Garabed were
much older than my father
because their mother was my
grandfather's first wife, and my
father and his sisters came from
his second wife.

Boghos, Garabed, & Armenag

Please note Boghos, because his daughter Manooshag, who will survive the massacre, will be the mother of Little Aram who will virtually steal Archie's paintings from me.

But you can forget Little Aram for now, and I will remind you of his lineage later.

Charlie, whose name in Armenian is Garabed, was actually named after the tall figure in the middle of the photo. Garabed and Boghos were children when our grandfather remarried, and Charlie's mother Nevart was born soon after, so I imagine Garabed was her favorite brother.

Archie's mother, Vartanoosh, was the next daughter after Nevart, and there was another daughter whom I know nothing about except that she was killed in the massacre; and then came my father who was the youngest son of the Najarian family, as I would be of what would remain of it in America.

The massacre, or what is now known as "the first genocide of the Twentieth Century," began in 1915; but the slaughter of Armenians had already started before then, and when Armenian young men were drafted as cannon fodder into the Turkish Army, some would flee abroad to France or America or wherever else they had a relative or sponsor.

Vartanoosh, Armenag & Nevart

This was how Charlie's father, Ohannes, and Archie's father, Hagop, had come to West Hoboken, where an Armenian community had settled among the other immigrants from Ireland and Italy and Germany.

Ohannes had been a neighbor of the Najarians back in Tigranakert, and he had written for Nevart to come as his wife. Then in 1910, when my father had turned seventeen and was about to be drafted, his older sister Vartanoosh sold her prized embroidery to escape with him and join Nevart and Ohannes in West Hoboken.

Needing to marry right away, since how else could a woman survive in the new world, Vartanoosh was soon hitched to Hagop, who was actually an in-law back in Tigranakert, and my father would remain under her wing even after the marriage.

Vartanoosh died before I was born, but according to my mother, she and my father were especially close, and in those days when the young immigrants were poor and crowded, it was only natural that her teenage brother would live with her and her new husband.

Fortunately Hagop was a mild mannered and passive man, while my father was supposed to have been a gentle man himself, and, according to my mother, my father soon became the breadwinner of the family, since Hagop wasn't up to the task.

Armen would even tell me my father was as much and sometimes even more a father to her than Hagop, and Archie had told me my father had bought him books and paid for his violin lessons and even got him his first job as a cartoonist with the local newspaper whose art editor was an Armenian.

I don't know why my father didn't marry and start a family of his own, but it may have had something to do with my mother falling in love with him after she married my brother's father, who was my father's second cousin.

I can hear you complain now about all these confusing connections, but please bear with me; they will soon end and I'll return to my main theme.

Like so many other girls who were orphaned by the

Zaroohe & Vartanoosh

massacre, my mother Zaroohe was a picture bride who entered the Najarian clan when her mother-in-law Annah brought her to America to marry Annah's son Vahan, who had fled here after escaping the draft.

Annah had also been an orphan who was adopted by my grandfather who was her maternal uncle, and she grew up with the Najarians until she married and had sons of her own.

In the meantime Annah was also related on her Pinajian side to Archie's father. So when my mother later divorced Annah's son and married my father who was Annah's first cousin, it was such a huge upheaval that a Tolstoi could have spun several novels about its aftermath; and I myself would try my hand at it in my own books.

It was actually my brother Tom who would first take me to Archie and Armen's home when I was about six, since I had never seen them because of Annah's ban when Archie's father had remained loyal to it.

Archie and Armen were Tom's cousins on his father's side, and my mother must have asked him to take me to visit them, though Tom was eleven years older than I and didn't usually like me tagging along with him.

And it may have been on that same Sunday when my mother put a nickel in my palm and asked me to say a prayer for my father in the little Armenian church that was on the way.

She herself never went to church, and though she had a deep faith in something bigger than herself, religion meant nothing to her.

She was however, like all peasants, a superstitious woman, and she put the nickel in my palm and told me to drop it in the little brass box by the candles and ask "Ahtz-vatz Dada," the heavenly father, to make my father well because she really believed it might do some good.

My father had been paralyzed by a stroke, and so it would happen that my praying for him would coincide with my adopting Archie as a father figure after my brother showed me the way to his home.

I didn't know then how close my father and Archie had been,

and after learning this I was confused about why Archie had never appeared in our home despite his father's loyalty to Annah's ban.

Armen, who was so fearful in so many other ways, would tell me she would secretly visit my father in those early days during my mother's divorce, and maybe Archie did too; and I probably never saw him in my infant years because he was in the Army when my father was stricken, so maybe he did come after his discharge when I was already in school.

But he never wanted to talk about such things, which was part of his character that I will unveil as my story unfolds, and the other part was the one I fell in love with.

* * *

Returning now to my movie, let's flashback to when I was a child visiting my cousin Archie.

I had just dropped my mother's nickel into the brass box by the candles, and staring up at the little painting over the flames that was either a Jesus or a Mary, I didn't believe that the painting or the church was part of what my mother called "Ahtz-vatz Dada," but like my mother I did believe in something bigger than myself. And I prayed to it as only a child can pray with the superstition that it was somehow tied to the flame of the candle I had just paid for.

"Please," I would whisper as deeply as I could, Sunday after Sunday for the next four years until he died: "please make my father better."

And then I would tiptoe out of the church to visit my cousin Archie, unaware that my prayer and my belief would be tied to the world of art that he would lead me to when I sat beside him with his arm around me as he read to me from a comic strip in the Sunday papers.

As far as I can remember it happened only once, but it would be as if it were all the time because of how deeply I had longed for my father to do the same.

And I remember to this day his index finger as he pointed to the pictures as he read the captions, because his nail was bent from having stuck it in a meat grinder when he too was a child, or so he said, while I too would grind meat for my own mother with the same kind of hand grinder you would screw to the seat of a wooden chair and then push the meat into the spirals with your index finger as you turned the handle.

And the captions in this particular comic strip were not in balloons but as in a book, because the strip was *Prince Valiant* that was still drawn in those days by the great Harold Foster who had illustrated Edgar Rice Burrough's *Tarzan* when Archie and Charlie were kids like me.

In fact they had loved Harold Foster so much they wanted to imitate him and become illustrators themselves, which was the same mimesis in how anyone becomes an artist.

Because making art was what being human was all about when it was not killing and stealing from each other, and we draw lines the way we sing and dance and learn to do it better by miming what we love.

And so it was that when my mother first met little "Ashod," as she called him in Armenian, in that March of 1921 when he had just turned seven and she had just arrived in his mother's kitchen from off the boat, he was scribbling with a pencil on the white porcelain table-top, and Vartanoosh had said in Armenian:

"There goes my little Ashod again, making more of his snakes."

And after the porcelain was wiped clean and the dinner was done he would make even more of them, since they were of course the snakes that wriggle in all of us.

And he would keep making them for the rest of his life, just like Harold Foster and every artist from all the way back to the caves.

And this was what the pictures in the panels of *Prince Valiant* were really about when he pointed with his bent fingernail at the warriors with swords and maidens in castles: it was the story of civilization itself that was the same kind of golden age and massacre that our parents had survived.

But I was too young to be aware of this of course, and as we sat on the old sofa by the potbelly stove in the little dusty parlor that he used for a studio, he himself was too caught in his love of anatomy and composition to think about anything else.

He had just returned from surviving another battleground where he had been a clerk behind the lines who may have recorded the names of the dead he never wanted to talk about, and I wouldn't know about it until a lifetime later when I called him one day and all he wanted to talk about was art when what I really wanted to know was the other side of it.

But his old age memory had forgotten its name.

"The Battle of the Bulge?" I asked.

"Yeh, the Battle of the Bulge," he said, as if it were ancient history by now.

And he didn't want to say anymore but to return to his painting that he kept piling in the dirt floor garage.

And so I end this first chapter of my book about him and Charlie as if it were a movie and I were a filmmaker who could flashback to watercolors and photographs and the necks of my two uncles sliced by sword like the sword of Prince Valiant and the dead frozen on a battlefield in Belgium and Vartanoosh like Andromache in her kitchen while the corpse of her Hector is dragged in the dust and my mute father sits alone with his paralyzed hand in his lap and a little Ashod is drawing his snakes like a cave man with a torch.

Enamel on paper, 1984

And so we flash back to when Archie and Charlie were kids who drew with chalk on the sidewalks while horses pulled the wagons of peddlers on the cobblestone streets.

And one Sunday, or so I imagine, they watched their uncle Armenag, my father, perform in an Armenian translation of a Shakespeare comedy in what was called a "*hantess*", which meant a togetherness with music and dance.

And it was held in a rented hall called "Swiss Turn Hall" because it had been a gym where the Swiss had turned with ropes and rings.

And it was around this time they met their new cousin Manooshag who had just arrived from Alexandria after her uncle Armenag sent her the fare for the boat.

She was a young woman by then, and she had survived the massacre when she was kidnapped as a slave by a band of Chechens after her father was beheaded, but how she escaped is too much to include here except that she will in a few years give birth to Little Aram who will one day virtually steal Archie's paintings from me.

In the meantime their much older cousin Annah has taken her young daughter-in-law, my mother, on a visit to Boston by a ferry from Long Island.

And in Boston was another survivor whose name was Vosdanig Adoian that he would change to Arshile Gorky, after the Greek hero Achilles and a Russian novelist.

And so I imagine Annah knew the Adoian family because my mother's artist brother was only twelve when he disappeared on the death march, and Gorky's famous painting of his mother and him was when Gorky was also around twelve.

Then leaving the hantess, little Archie and Charlie drew with chalk because of what old Carnig Shenloogian once told me after Archie had died:

"Sure I remember your cousin Archie," Carnig said. "He used to entertain us with his cartoons on the sidewalk when we were kids."

The sidewalks were slabs of slate in those days, and in my own as well, and the slate must have come from the cliffs of the Palisades where they had moved in West New York that was more upscale, though it was just a short trolley ride from where they were born.

The prosperity of the Jazz Age had trickled down to where Armenag could sell his jewelry and move Vartanoosh and her family near Nevart's, who had come to West New York after Charlie's father made good money as a photoengraver, so the two cousins were still near each other in their early teens.

Then one day Charlie's father took him to the Metropolitan Museum where he saw the huge painting called *Washington Crossing the Delaware* by Emmanuel Gottlieb Leutze, 1816-1868, which you can see on Google.

And it moved him so deeply he realized all he wanted was to learn how to paint such a great picture of such a great subject that would move others in the same way.

And he would tell me this in the Met a lifetime later after Archie had died and I had come back east with the slides of Archie's paintings I had salvaged in search of where to show them.

We were resting in the comfortable wicker chairs in the new American Wing, and it was actually the first time I really came to love him as I did Archie who had been my father figure, since I had seen Charlie so rarely in our long lives when I had been gone for so long.

Charlie's wife Edna had passed away and his kids had moved out west, and though he was eighty-three by now he had outlasted me in our tour of the galleries where he still couldn't get his fill of them.

And he said as we sat looking at *Washington Crossing The Delaware:*

"You know, kid," he always called me kid though I was sixty by now, "this is not a museum to me; I come here like coming to church."

* * *

And now we flash back to Archie himself crossing the Hudson on a ferry in my own version of the Leutze painting on what could have been the very day Charlie first saw it as a kid.

Archie was three years older than Charlie and had just graduated from high school after skipping two grades, and he had found
a job as a clerk in a carpet factory in lower Manhattan.

It was now 1930 and the job had come just when his father and
his uncle Armenag were suddenly out of work, and he had become
the sole breadwinner though he was only sixteen.

And so crossing the river like Washington facing the future of
America, he sat in the rear of the ferry where the froth of the wake
flowed backwards like history, and the snakes he had scribbled as a
child now reached to imitate his heroes as he studied in an anatomy
book how each muscle fit into another.

Because there was no other kind of art in America in those
days, though Arshile Gorky was about to find a new one in the studio he just rented in lower Manhattan that could have been around
the corner from the carpet factory.

The only art the young Archie knew, however, was where he
had to learn anatomy like every other artist since the caves when
the anatomy was of an animal, and he had that same need to learn
it that kept his spirit alive in the ten hour factory days when the
only time he could draw was on the ferry and at night.

Look at him now on one of those nights when he sits buried in
his lines while his uncle Armenag twists silver into jewelry no one
will buy and his mother Vartanoosh is dying from intestinal cancer.

What was his mother like, I once asked him. But all he would
say was:

"She was a good woman; she left me alone to do whatever I
wanted."

And that was all he would ever tell me, just as he would never
tell me what was deepest inside him except his love of making lines,
though my mother would tell me she was there that day Vartanoosh
died when he had just come home from work.

"And when Ashod came through the door and I told him she
was gone, he fainted and fell to the floor."

* * *

He had been, my mother would say, so full of energy as a child that he would stammer when he tried to speak, as if his tongue could not open all that wanted to come out.

And he was, she would say, just like Vartanoosh whom everyone loved for her gentle nobility, and his love of lines would be like her beautiful lace.

She too had a quick wit, but she too could be reserved and silent, and she suffered without a word wearing a sac at her side for the drip of what little she ate when there was no money for a doctor or medicine.

And her suffering, like the Depression itself, drove him deeper into his lines where he would turn it into a world of comics like a wish-fulfillment of a golden age.

It was the Golden Age of Illustration in the middle of the Depression, from the word *illustrare*, to make bright, and he drew a series called *That 'Ol Gang O'Mine* as if it were an American

version of where his uncle Armenag performed in a Shakespeare pastoral and the survivors would never mention the massacre again.

Because that was what art was really all about, it was dancing away the great depression and selling his lines to a magazine for the bread of life to stay alive, and so he kept drawing them at night while the factory swallowed his youth and his mother died in pain like Arshile Gorky's.

* * *

In the meantime Charlie's father Ohannes was still making good money as a photoengraver while so many others were out of work, and Ohannes finally said okay, he would pay for the art school called Pratt if that's what his son Charlie really wanted.

And so Charlie too rode the ferry across the river to where he studied the anatomy every artist needed to know to make the world bright, and he loved it so deeply he would teach it in Pratt himself one day.

It was not just anatomy of course, it was how Washington crossed into the future of America, and then one day he met the great Norman Rockwell who was the king of painting the American pastoral.

Charlie was a senior by then, and by chance he was sent to meet Rockwell at Grand Central Station and lead him to a lecture at Pratt, and Rockwell had forgotten his wallet and wrote Charlie an I.O.U. for the fare to Brooklyn.

Charlie's daughter Gwen told me this just the other day when I called her in Sacramento where she had seen a Rockwell retrospective, but all she could remember was that Rockwell agreed to answer any question after the lecture except how much money he made, and she had no idea what happened to that I.O.U.

* * *

And so the two cousins survived The Great Depression, and one night when Archie saw the movie *Scarface* he was inspired to create a comic book he called *Gangsters' Guns*, or so he once told me, but it must have been a re-run of *Scarface*, which came out in

1932, and comic books came later.

He had moved by now with his father and sister back to West Hoboken that had joined with Union Hill to become Union City, and he was creating one comic book after another.

"He was always a prodigious reader," Charlie would tell me, and when they were kids, "he wanted to be a writer as much as an artist," so comic books were right up his alley where he could imagine stories to his heart's content and give rein to his lines at the same time.

"Down the block," he himself would tell me, which must have meant where he delivered his panels in Manhattan, "someone came out with Superman," but he didn't take any notice because he was in his own world of cops and robbers.

His uncle Armenag had married my mother by now, and my brother Tom who was a kid then, would remember posing for Archie's comic book called "Reynolds of the Royal Mounted."

That comic is lost now, and I attach one from a few years later,

called *Invisible Justice*, in which Archie used one of his pseud-onyms, "Art Gordon."

* * *

Charlie too began drawing comic books after he graduated, though someone else wrote the stories, and he was drawing a series called *Lady Luck* when he was one of the first to be drafted in 1940 before the war was to begin.

His uncle Armenag, my father, took the bus to Fort Dix to see him, and years later when Charlie told me this I said:

"He must have been worried about you."

"Of course he worried about me, I was his sister's son."

He was in an artillery outfit that was being sent to the Pacific, but his sergeant in the barracks sent his drawings to a contest for servicemen in Life Magazine, and his drawings won first prize.

And when they were published one of the brass happened to come to Life to hire artists to draw manuals in Washington, and the editor pointed to Charlie's prize-winner saying:

"Why don't you hire one of your own?"

And so Charlie was sent to Washington as if by Lady Luck, while his outfit went to the Pacific where who knows how many were killed?

In the meantime another genocide was started by the Nazis like the one our parents had escaped, and in America Norman Rockwell was painting an American pastoral while Arshile Gorky painted the portrait of his mother who starved to death in Armenia.

"Take Cover" is Private Charles Mazoujian's exciting sketch of soldiers unloading from a truck convoy while being strafed by a swarm of low-flying enemy planes. Artist Mazoujian says he memorized the scenes on this page from actual maneuvers in which he and his battery participated.

IN "BEACH DEFENSE" SOLDIERS ARE SHOWN PRACTICING TO REPEL A SEA INVASION

NEW SOLDIER ART

For those soldiers and sailors whose hobby is art, the Hobby Guild of America recently sponsored an art contest on "Our Life in the Service." A large majority of the 600 contestants were Army men because sailors have found that a pitching boat is no fit place to draw or paint. Best of the work submitted is now being sent on a 40-week tour of 40 cities, where it will be exhibited mostly in department stores and service clubs. On the next pages LIFE presents paintings by four soldiers who demonstrate that the new mechanized Army, with its trucks, guns, tanks and airplanes, as well as the simple things of camp life, can be inspiring subjects for dramatic and forthright art. From time to time LIFE will publish more examples of art by men in the armed forces.

On this page are five drawings by a star contestant, 24-year-old Charles Mazoujian of New Jersey, born of Armenian parentage. Under the name Ford Davis, Mazoujian was the creator of a cartoon strip called "Lady Luck." Now he is a member of a Coast Artillery battery, a railroad unit known in the Army as the "Iron Horse" boys, stationed on the U. S. East Coast.

"Depress!" shows a gun crew loading a 12-in. mortar and maneuvering it into firing position on a mobile railway mount. Below: Taking A Break, says the artist, shows "boys just returned from a 10-mile march brooding over the fact that blistered feet caused them to break a heavy date."

IN "NIGHT MARCH" TROOPS HURRY TO ANTI-AIRCRAFT GUNS TO WARD OFF PLANES

Charlie's drawings in Life Magazine

Art and War

Archie's original drawing for the Army magazine, The Marksman, *while he was in boot camp in Texas. It was reproduced in the Dallas Morning News, Sept. 12, 1943*

The war ended the Depression, and after Archie was drafted he was sent to a boot camp in Texas where one of his buddies in the barracks was another artist whom he would call "Avati."

James Avati, 1912 to 2005, whose work can be seen on Google, would become one of the most famous illustrators of pocket book covers after the war, and by chance he had retired in Petaluma, so I was able to drive there to interview him after Archie died.

Yes, he said, he remembered my cousin, "the philosopher," who would crack everyone up in the barracks with his humor, but he was sorry he could recall no more and they never saw each other again after the war.

Archie however would remember Avati "introducing" him to "fine art" when Avati had wanted to be a fine artist himself, and as I was visiting Archie one day when I was a kid he had just bought a new paperback of *The Invisible Man*, and he said to me:

"Look! Another cover by Avati! He wanted to be a fine artist and I wanted to be an illustrator, and now he's an illustrator and I'm into fine art!"

I attach a pencil sketch of a figure called "Jimmy" who must be Avati sketching in his own pad. It was in the pile of Archie's war drawings that I found after he died, and according to the date, September '44, it must have been before they were separated in France.

Avati told me he was trained as a technician while Archie was to be a scout, and scouts were the first to be killed on the battlefield, but Lady Luck would save him just as she had saved Charlie.

"*Jimmy*"

Charlie, who had become a warrant officer because of his drawings, had failed to get Archie to Washington as an artist, and Archie was to be sent abroad as a scout when his outfit suddenly lost their clerk and he was the replacement because he had been a clerk in the carpet factory.

And so instead of being killed at the front he was behind

Archie on furlough from boot camp, with Charlie in D.C.

the lines, where I imagine he recorded the names of the dead instead of being one of them.

But he would never tell me anything else about the war, though my mother would tell me his father had told her he once had to stand in a river all day with nothing to eat but a Hershey bar, which must have been during the battle of the Bulge that I wouldn't know about until I mentioned it to him in one of my phone calls before he died.

Archie and Charlie by the sea near D.C.

Nor did he ever tell me about his bronze medal that was found buried in the attic, and who knows what it was for? My friend Leo Litwak, who was in the Bulge himself and wrote one of the finest memoirs of war, *The Medic*, told me that in his own outfit his superior officer awarded a bronze medal to a favorite so he wouldn't be sent to Japan at the war's end in Europe.

And I would learn little else about Archie in the war except from the few letters he wrote to his sister as he marched from France to Holland and into Germany, where he must have witnessed what he never wanted to talk about.

But then no art could tell the true horror of any war, and like Goya's Disasters it would be doomed to illustration if it tried.

I imagine he had known the limits of art since he first began drawing his comics while his mother was dying, and he would know these limits more than ever as he drew the little Dutch kids who asked for food and the German soldier raising his arms who could have killed one of his buddies.

I found the drawings with the leftovers of his comics in an old cardboard box buried by his rotting canvasses in the garage in Bellport, and they're here now buried under my own canvasses that may also rot someday.

Those who now own Archie's paintings want to make a big deal of his war history as if it might entice a rich collector to buy them, but he had no wish to make any use of it when he was alive.

According to his discharge paper that was in his box of drawings, he was inducted in "9 Nov 42" and discharged "13 Jan 46," as a "cpl" and "clerk typist 405" in "407 INF REGT HQ CO," and his decorations were: "AMERICAN THEATER VICTORY MEDAL EUROPEAN AFRICAN-MIDDLE EASTER RIBBON GOOD CONDUCT MEDAL BRONZE STAR MEDAL GO100 HQ 102 INF 15 JUL 45."

However in one of his drawings of himself with a pipe that he never smoked he mentions wearing also a "COMBAT INFANTRY MEDAL.

The following are excerpts from the eight letters to his sister that he had typed around his sketches, which are in photocopies called V-MAIL:

"Bonjour Armen and Pa: Just read your letter dated Sept 24, Sunday. It's your first letter and boy was I glad to hear from you. Glad to hear everything is well and Uncle is improving steadily. [Re: my father's stroke]. I am feeling fine and getting used to France. Am trying to make sketches of French towns and will send you some. Here is one of myself in a typical ritual — CHOW! Well, by now you must have received my several V-mails. They state what I need. Hope you will take care of them. Regards to you all.

"Dear Sis, just a little mememto of our trip into Europe. I made this on a Sunday's sketching trip with Jimmy [Avati]. The original drawing [see attached: Sketched at Fermanville, France Oct 44] was in Wolff [carbon] pencil. Then I copied it onto this V-MAIL. Several of the villagers stopped to watch and converse with us, saying "Tres Bon!" (I made out fairly well in my French)....P.S. Try to get some Wolff Carbon pencils from Macy's and hurry them along. Down to my last stub.

"Sketched at Fermanville, France"

"Somewhere in France 19 October 1944....It's been sometime since I heard from you last. Hope you and Pa are all right. I am fine and taking things in stride. Have been sketching quite a lot of children following us asking for "BONBONS!" and chewing gum, all of them rosy cheeked. In fact all of the inhabitants have plenty of color on their faces. I went through one of the villages the other day. It was a quaint town full of rickety houses and thatched roofs. The streets are crooked and winding. There are no stores like ours. They are shops with no signs or neons. They remind me of Dickens' stories and their locale. I hope you received my letters requesting fixative, pads, etc. at Macy's. You should be able to get Wolff's Carbon drawing pencils which are made in England. I wish you can send as many as you can get as I am continually using them. This is very important! Hope you can send them immediately.Give all my regards to Pa and also to Uncle. Tell him to get well soon as some day we will all come home and start all over again. Give him my regards and tell Tommy to write. [My father's stroke was in January of 1944.]

"Somewhere in Holland. Just received your Vees of Nov 12 and 15....also one of your packages and am anxiously awaiting the others, especially with the art materials as I can start making

some portraits when I get the fixative. Too bad you did not get those Wolff pencils as they are my favorite. PLEASE TRY AGAIN AS I CAN CERTAINLY MAKE OUT BETTER WITH THEM. Otherwise I will have to use WASH, which is too much trouble in working. Here are Dutch children standing around while we are eating, waiting for leftovers….P.S.Send me a tube of Chinese White, Lamp Black, (watercolor, not oil) CHARCOAL STUBS, BOTTLES OF BLACK INK.

"MERRY CHRISTMAS from somewhere in Holland, drawing] 4 nov/44…am sending my Xmas greetings early this year just in case….

"Somewhere in Germany! 11 Dec 44….Presenting herewith (with myself as inspiration) a combat soldier of the ETO (European Theater of Operations)….the little medal

on his chest is a COMBAT INFANTRY MEDAL...the pipe has not been [and will never be] lighted so hold up on your tobacco....Am running low on ink, white paint (have none) and V-Mail forms....

"Somewhere in Germany 10 Jan. 1945....A self-portait is difficult here due to the fact that this was drawn from memory and it is so long that I have seen myself realistically....Have seen a Rockwell

cover, a late Cosmopolitan with drawings from the South Pacific by Bundy, and also a Morgan drawing....You can forward this to Charlie for my first self-portait on V-Mail.....

"Somewhere in Germany 5 March 1945. Here is a sketch of some locomotives....used the fountain pen you sent...."

ADDITIONAL WAR DRAWINGS & V-MAILS:

On the troop ship to England.

Clerks at work in tent. Oct 15, 44 Theville, France

"The Road to ———."! Nov 44

Straddle Trench

This is the ETO! [European Theater Operations]

German Soldier Surrendering

War Devastation

[Untitled watercolor, location unknown]

****

In the meantime, while Archie was marching across the battlefields and Charlie was in Washington, Arshile Gorky had discovered a new kind of art that he and his younger rivals like de Kooning and Pollack would push further after the war ended.

And this new art would appear in my childhood as if it were the end of all illustration, and I would grow up with it as I did with the Bomb of Hiroshima and the Nazi concentration camps that would be like the end of history itself.

I turned five when the war ended in August of 1945, and I would remember the air filled with confetti as I stood on Bergenline Avenue looking up to where my father sat at the window looking down at me, and a new world would open like the mushroom of a nuclear explosion.

The end of the war was the beginning of my memory, and the new art that appeared in my cousin Archie's little parlor where I would visit him after I prayed for my father would be like the air filled with confetti while my father sat with his paralyzed hand in his lap and Arshile Gorky would soon hang himself.

It was all happening then that I struggle now to compose and condense as if this little chapter about art and war could be a canvas like Gorky's and his rivals' that Archie was just discovering then.

And it may have even been Charlie who introduced it to him, or so Charlie would tell me a lifetime later.

Charlie had returned to Brooklyn to live with Edna's parents, and he was hired to teach life study and painting by George McNeill in the night school at Pratt.

And George McNeill (see Google) had also hired his other friends, Franz Kline and Philip Guston and Jacob Lawrence who were not famous then, and Charlie hung out with them and even went with McNeil one night to the Cedar Tavern where he may have met de Kooning.

Archie in the meantime had known nothing of them around the time he was reading to me from Prince Valiant and drawing a comic book of Hopalong Cassidy.

But he had no feeling for comics anymore, he would tell me years later, and like so many veterans returning from the battlefields, he felt "adrift."

He was around thirty-two when I first visited him in my need of a father figure, and we were each actually growing up together in a world of art where he would adopt me as a kind of sidekick in his discoveries.

He discovered, he would later tell me, that he didn't know what art really was before then, and ironically it was Avati who pointed the way when all he had known was the illustration while

Avati wanted to be a fine artist.

Then in his love of reading he came across Irving Stone's biography of Van Gogh, *Lust For Life*, and it moved him very deeply.

And so do I write about him now like Stone wrote about Van Gogh, though I can only imagine what he really meant by his word "adrift." All biography is really a kind of fiction, especially autobiography, and vice-versa, so what I give you now is only what I can imagine.

The war had awakened him while it sent so many others asleep, and he may have felt like when I was thirty-two and felt as if I were waking from a nightmare and didn't know what was real anymore.

His father and sister were working by the time the war ended, and the Depression was gone and there was no worry about rent or food, so he could make use of the G.I. Bill and enrolled in the Art Students League across the river in Manhattan.

It was, I see now, around the same time Arshile Gorky would hang himself, and I use the two events for what my story is about to unfold, though Archie didn't know anything about Gorky then.

He knew only illustrators like Rockwell, and he enrolled in the League because he thought it would help him become an illustrator like Rockwell, but no sooner did he start painting at the League that he realized no, he didn't want to be an illustrator, he wanted to be an artist like Van Gogh, and yet what was really the difference?

And the question of the difference was what he would keep filling in my ears as I sat on the couch watching him hop around his easel like the simian Picasso who was soon to become his new hero.

And this would be a crucial scene of the movie I would like to film for you: myself at the age of nine watching my father figure show me his canvasses while he pontificated about the difference between illustration and fine art, as if I had become a Sancho Panza to his Quixote as he held his brush in his hand like a lance.

Who was my cousin Archie? What kind of man would talk to a child as if that child could really understand what he was talking about? He wasn't of course really talking to me, just as so many parents don't really talk to their children as much as they need to be heard.

Look at us now as I sit on the couch and watch him teach me about the meaning of art when he was just beginning to learn it himself, as if he himself was still that child who once stammered when his tongue couldn't open all that was inside him.

It is 1949 and the painting on his easel has replaced the Hopalong Cassidy panels on the drawing board by the potbelly stove, and the redolence of the paint and gum turpentine follow the frankincense and candlewax in the little church where I was still praying for my father to be whole again.

And now look at him alone, as if my love for him could be a movie:

He is waiting at the same bus stop where my father had his stroke years before, which was only a few blocks away from his home with his sister and father; and the ferry is gone and the bus through the new tunnel takes only a few minutes to the new Port Authority Terminal from where he will walk to the League.

The busses from the suburbs to Manhattan run all day and night, and they each must pass by the last bus stop in Union City, so the wait for any one of them is never more than a few minutes.

Then as the bus curves to the mouth of the Lincoln tunnel that was just built in the previous years, it passes the rocks of the cliff the engineers had to bore, and the slabs of slate are the same as the sidewalks Archie once chalked for his pals.

He was a city kid, but the rocks and the little sumac trees that grew between them were always close, and we must look close at these rocks and trees for what my movie will reveal, because their lines and planes are the same as in the canvasses of the new art that was to be the end of the golden age of illustration and was in turn itself an illustration of the world after Hiroshima and the concentration camps.

Germany '45 [Possibly a concentration camp?]

Art and Illustration

I *n the meantime* Charlie was not adrift but at the peak of his talent with watercolors like the one that had won a national prize.

He gave a similar watercolor as a gift to my mother after she stayed a week with his little Craig in his new home in Tenafly when Edna was giving birth to baby Gwen in the hospital while Charlie was working and teaching.

I've always loved this watercolor, I would tell him fifty years later when we looked at it in my mother's home one day, and he would say like an old athlete who had long retired:

"I can't do that anymore."

Yet back in the old days he had played with the pros until he could afford the move to Tenafly, and I return there now to when he came to the bus stop in his new '51 Studebaker to drive us to his new home that he had just built.

And while my mother and Armen chatted with Edna upstairs, I stood with him and Archie in his little studio in the basement

Watercolor by Charlie, circa 1951 (Color affected by reproduction)

with the window looking out to the woods, and it was the first time I was together with my father's nephews who I imagined were like him.

My father had died the year before, and no longer praying for him in the little church, I had a new church in the world of art, and though I myself would not be a painter for years to come, I had already written my first story after O. Henry's *The Last Leaf* about how much painting meant to me.

Painting, painting, and more painting, was all my father figure cousins wanted to talk about, and standing with them in the basement studio I listened as they looked at the illustrations in books and magazines by artists in *The Famous Artists School* that was in those days even advertised inside free packs of cigarette matches.

The Famous Artists School, according to Wikipedia, had been started a few years earlier in 1948 by Albert Dorne after Dorne's conversation with Norman Rockwell, and for the faculty Dorne recruited (in alphabetical order):

"John Atherton, Austin Briggs, Steven Dohanos, Robert Fawcett, Peter Helck, Fred Ludekens, Al Parker, Norman Rockwell, Ben Stahl, Harold Von Schmidt, and Jon Whitcomb.

"All were making more than $50,000 a year, equal to $450,000 today, and later faculty included Cowboy Artist Harvey Johnson and cartoonists Roger Vernon, Al Capp, Milton Caniff, and Rube Goldberg, and advisory faculty later included Stuart Davis, Ben Shawn, Fletcher Martin, Ernest Fiene, Arnold Blanch, and Doris Lee."

Yet who would remember those names now that were then as popular as rock stars, and as I stood with Charlie and Archie in that little basement studio, even the Golden Age of Illustration was already dying.

And "it was television that would kill it," Charlie would tell me years later, meaning not only the paintings in magazines that had been his bread and butter, but the magazines themselves.

He would survive a few more years with his freelance work and his part-time teaching, but by the end of the Fifties he would have to commute to a nine to five job in an advertising agency of Ogilvy and Mather on Madison Avenue, drawing storyboards to support his family, and his devotion to painting would be left behind for evenings and weekends.

Archie, however, was just beginning then to learn about the new action painting he was only just discovering, though he still loved the old kind that he and Charlie were talking about that Sunday, especially Von Schmidt's, whose horses they both loved in the illustrations for western stories.

To paint a horse in motion was as exciting as riding one, yet as Charlie was being pulled away from his easel to support his family, Archie was being pulled from his old love for illustration.

And though I was only eleven I was at his side like a sidekick as he was about to turn in the fork in the road to where he would never turn back.

It was a momentous Sunday I want to show you now, because it was not just the turning point between illustration and fine-art, but what they each signified.

What was the realism in the old art and what was the new one called abstract? What in fact was painting itself and the reality of family life with children and mortgages? Was a painting only paint while flesh and blood was life and death?

I was only eleven, but I was in the twilight of my puberty where I was about to wake from my first wet dream that would be like the crack in the cosmic egg, and the new painting would mirror it like a nuclear explosion.

Born in the beginning of the war, I was of the generation that would be the first to grow up with what everyone now takes for granted, though it didn't exist before then, and the new action painting that evolved in New York during the war would soon supplant the classical realism that had evolved from Fifth Century Athens.

And so we flash forward to 1953, when I played hooky from seventh grade one morning to go with Archie on his Friday tour of the galleries, and though I can't remember why I chose that particular Friday and had no idea of what to expect, I remember that being with him had become more important than school, and that morning would be like an epiphany.

Manhattan had always been since the dawn of my memory like an enchanted fairyland from where I would gaze at its skyline whenever I played on the cliffs, and the Empire State Building would rise from it like the sun itself rising behind it.

Manhattan was where my father once worked at his jewelry in his shop on 46th Street that is now actually named Jewelry Street, and I was actually passing it with my father figure Archie on that Friday morning, though I wasn't aware of this then.

In fact it now blurs like a dream where we walked all the way from the Port Authority Terminal to 57th Street where he showed me the studio in the Art Students League.

He painted only a few years at the League, but he would later mention that one of the instructors in the workshops was Byron Browne, who like Gorky had pioneered the new art he was about to explore while he still had one foot in the old one of illustration.

"You're a landscape painter, Pinajian," Browne told him one day, but this was before he went to Woodstock and Browne must have referred to his imaginary landscapes and not any in plein air.

And so looking back, I see now that what his exploring really meant was not only the difference between what he imagined and what he would call "nature," but it was like asking what the Buddha meant in the Heart Sutra about form and emptiness.

What is it we see in our mind's eye and what is really out there?

Painting then was not only about what would sell in a gallery or compete with other painters, it was facing the nature of form itself, and this would be his life-long quest that he would share with me like Don Quixote shared his own with Sancho Panza, and like Quixote Archie would die in it as well.

But that was yet to come, and we were now walking from the League to Madison Avenue while passing where Charlie would soon be working in Oglivy and Mather, and we continued to the gallery where I was about to have an epiphany.

I had never been to a gallery before, and when we came to the one called the Sidney Janis that was uptown in those days, it was like an empty shop whose walls were painted white.

Then as we entered I was struck by its emptiness and silence as if it were a kind of chapel whose icons were now paintings, and the silence felt so deep we would have to whisper as if it were holy.

And no one was there except two men standing in the rear by the desk where they talked so softly I could barely hear them; and as I stood with Archie looking at one of the works on the wall, Archie leaned to my ear and whispered:

"That's de Kooning over there, talking with Janis."

And I suddenly felt as if I had entered another realm like the boy Percival in the chapel of the grail where the real and the unreal had suddenly merged.

I had never heard of de Kooning before, and hardly anyone else did either, since this was one of his first solo exhibits; nor of course did I know anything of Percival except the world he shared with Prince Valiant in Harold Foster's comic strip.

But at that magical age of falling in love with heroes, I saw a short man about Archie's height who was built solid and squat like Archie, and like Archie he had finely chiseled features, though unlike Archie he was not bald but had fine white hair that seemed to glow.

And I wanted to rush to him and tell him how we were some-how related in a realm called art that had taken the place of the church where I had prayed for my father:

You don't know me, I wanted to say, but my cousin Archie is also an artist and we are really a kind of family and....

And what? What was it that was rushing inside me when all I would remember next was leaving the gallery and walking back down the avenue in a kind of trance?

Nor would I remember anything of the work on the wall but that it was a new art I didn't understand and that Archie was just beginning to understand himself.

And it wouldn't be until a lifetime later that I would see those same works in an exhibit in the San Francisco Museum of Modern Art, called *Tracing the Figure*, where in the pentimenti of the slash-es and erasures you may see on Google why that epiphany in my puberty was a kind of prophecy of my own slashes and erasures.

And just as Percival would never find the grail again but would keep searching for it for the rest of his life, so too would I search in the rest of my life for what I am now trying to show you, as if this chapter could pierce an illusion in the same way de Kooning had pierced the figures of illustration.

The Sidney Janis Gallery was of course not a chapel, nor was Archie and de Kooning the saints of my hero worship, though they too would devote their lives to the same search as Percival's.

And so too would the magical innocence of that morning lead me to what Blake once called the realm of experience in the prophecy of *The Four Zoas* that he would never publish:

What is the price of experience?
 do men buy it for a song?
Or wisdom for a dance in the street? No,
 it is bought with the price
Of all that a man hath, his house, his wife, his
 children.
Wisdom is sold in the desolate market where
 none come to buy,
And in the wither'd field where the farmer
 plows for bread in vain.

* * *

And so I turn now to the next scene in that same year when Charlie was still struggling to pay his mortgage with his freelance work.

He had a job illustrating for a magazine, and like Gericault once asked the young Delacroix to pose for his *Raft of Medusa*, he asked Archie and me to come with Edna to a photographer's studio for some scenes in a story, and I attach here now the photo of Edna holding my hand and another of Archie twisting on the floor as if in pain.

It reminds me of what my mother once told me she heard about Archie from his father, who had found him writhing on the floor one day because the pain in his arm was too severe for him to

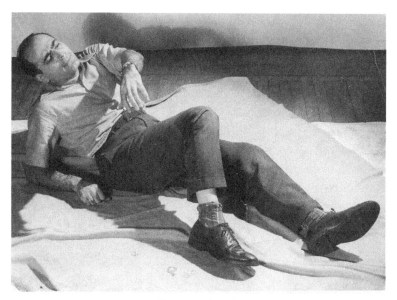

Archie Posing for Charlie

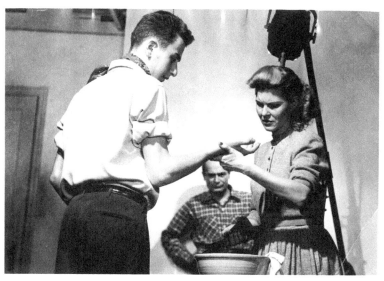

Pete, Archie and Edna

continue drawing his Hopalong Cassidy panels.

I would ask him about this in the last conversation I had with him before he died, and he would shrug it away saying it was just a pain, and anyway, he said, he could have drawn with his other hand because like my father he was ambidextrous.

Nevertheless my mother's story would stay with me as if that pain in his arm were somehow tied to his leaving the money and security of his Hopalong Cassidy for the fork in the road where there was no turning back.

And so I attach the little life study he painted of me around the time of the the photographer's studio, where you can see the influence of Picasso in the same way Picasso influenced Gorky and de Kooning.

He painted this life study in less than an hour one Sunday afternoon while I stood leaning with my arm on the mantle behind the potbelly stove in the parlor of the apartment in Union City. It was in the winter after he returned from his summer in Woodstock where his new life of action painting had just begun.

Archie's life study of Pete, circa 1954

Art and Nature

I *don't know how* Archie discovered Woodstock, probably from friends in the League, nor do I know much of his life outside my own, especially his sex life and how he could be so happy while never marrying when why I didn't made me so miserable.

But unlike me he was blessed with what we call a good nature, as in the Armenian word for both the wide open spaces and our characters: *pin-new-tiun.*

And since he was a virile and good-looking man who was also blessed with a quick wit like his mother, finding a mate would have been much easier for him than it was for me.

I first realized this when turning nineteen in the summer of 1959, I drove my '47 Chevy to see him in Woodstock, and not expecting me he said:

"I'm really sorry, kid, but I got invited for dinner with someone tonight. You know how it is, so don't wait up for me."

Then I watched as he washed his armpits in the little sink in the toilet and powdered them with talc for whatever might happen after dinner.

And so I fried a hamburger for myself on his hotplate as I would back in college, and then I slept on the old mattress on the floor with the windows open to the cool delicious mountain air and the soothing rhythm of the crickets.

It was in a loft above a barn that seemed to smell of the hay for whatever had been below, and there was only the tiny toilet with the tiny sink, so he had to bathe in the creek across the road or shower at the League's summer studio nearby; and I could see how happy he must have been in such a place as long as he wanted nothing else, which of course was the secret of all happiness.

Yet how he could be happy without a wife and family like Charlie's was beyond me in those days, until I too began to paint and realized how absorbed he was in his work and what it was about.

There was of course some loneliness and the usual gloomy thoughts that came with being human, but they would pass and there would always be what had kept him going since he was a kid scribbling snakes on the palimpsest of his mother's porcelain table.

He did love women and had a healthy lust for them, but he wouldn't let it get in his way, just as he had said when I asked him one day if he had ever been in love, and he said:

"There was a girl in the carpet factory, but I never did anything about it."

But that was during the Depression and the grinding poverty that had devoured his youth like his mother's cancer, and the rest would be like the dark ages of his personal history where who knew what he really felt and did?

There were prostitutes of course, and he even offered me the name of one when I was moaning about my sexual misery one day; and then there were the occasional nights like the one when he powdered his armpits, but as far as I know he was never in love with anyone after the girl in the carpet factory, and when I asked him one day what he did with his lust, he said:

"I put it all in my work."

I would do the same of course, though I was not as happy about it, nor did I have a nature that was the same word as what I prayed to as a child for my father to be whole again.

Nature was of course not just the realm of the unknowable, but what he was trying to find in the vanishing point of his compositions, and the quest would never end as if for the holy grail itself.

What was art and what was nature, and what was the difference while the mountain loomed behind the little barn and the creek flowed through the woods?

* * *

And so I flashback to the first of his letters, which I have edited and re-formatted.

The very first was in reply to my own letters, and he had changed the name of Woodstock to Stockwood, as in the novel he had just begun, which he called The Model and The Mountain.

Stockwood, July 16, 1955

Dear Bid, [from Biddo, my family nickname for Bedros that I signed in my letters] I was supposed to type this but the machine is broken [an Underwood portable like the one he used as a clerk during the war], first time in 17 years, so am scrawling this and hope it is readable.

"Enjoyed your letter immensely, all the comments, ideas, school troubles, etc. The same thing happened to me. [Turning fifteen I was about to learn French in my sophomore year]. That's when your father bought me the French dictionary, which you may have when you start....

"I'm always glad I took French as it tied in with my art career; it makes things interesting when you know a few words that can make you part of another world....The broader your interest the happier you will be, since everything is related at one time or another, though it may not seem so at the moment.

"Life is not lived all at once, it goes on and on and you are living it every day. You cannot know everything at once, and it is bad if you did, because you might then burn yourself out.

"The steady learning into the older years is the way I think it was intended. In the meantime you live, have fun, wait for the answers to the problems you have at the moment, and the answers will come.

"It is only by waiting and searching that they do come. To some people when they are young, to some when they are older, and some very old. The fact that it does come is a result of living a happy, healthy life, the ingredients of course are being happy within yourself, contentment with what you have at the moment and making up your mind to do better.

To wish for something you do not have will burn yourself out, overbalance your life and crowd everything into a shorter life. This to me is what happened to men like London and Van Gogh, men of great talent who for some reason or another worked furiously and intensely.

"I guess they had to do it because of a powerful drive, yet we know of so many great artists who also succeeded in later years and went on to getting better and better. Great work will always come out if desire is there and knowledge is behind it.

"Your understanding of life and your attitude is what creates knowledge. A confused person will produce a confused work because his knowledge is not clear. My constant searching has always given me the way to understanding why my pictures lack certain qualities. In other words, I had always to wait in line to find out what I lacked.

"The answer to what I did wrong last year is apparent this year. Patience is important. Sometimes you want to be something you aren't so people will think well of you. It just isn't there and you have to wait. In the meantime you keep working and hoping you will get over the difficulties.

"These difficulties will iron themselves out if you forget about them, though of course you can't really forget, for they are inside you, waiting to be overcome; often they are overcome while you are walking or sleeping or reading or listening to music, since all these are part of living and related to your problems. Teaching cannot go this far, for the person must experience his difficulty to surmount it.

"I thought I would put this down as it is some of what keeps me going. I am having a very nice time painting and living up here. The weather lately has turned hot and humid and I have to go swimming. During June it was very cold so I did more work.

"I am still improving. I have to be careful, as there are plenty of pictures and artists up here and each sings a different tune. To know your own tune and to try to stick to it while everyone else is beating their own chest is difficult. I have to know what is good and what isn't, which sometimes gets baffling, so I have to remain with the masters. They had great discipline and this is the most important thing in art.

"I haven't done much these past two weeks, but again I will have to wait for things to happen and am not worried about it. Actually my mind is resting and I will gradually get back to fresher pastures.

"What are you doing and where are you going on your days off? The chorag your Ma sent was terrific. [An Armenian pastry flavored with fennel and nigella seeds, pronounced chor-eg in proper Armenian, chor-ag in the Tigranakerttsi dialect. It is still tasty after it dries, when it can be dunked in tea or coffee.] Really enjoyed them. Thank her a lot.... Also my regards to Tom [my brother] and his fiancee.

"I will try to get back to the city for a day or two, since there is a terrific show at the Modern. However I must find someone driving down. [He never learned how to drive and would always depend on Charlie or Tom or his friend from the League, Paul Becker.]

"Well, I had better close now since it is getting hot and I have to go swimming. Also I am invited to dinner at someone's house in the evening. A terrific day and back to work tomorrow; hope I do better things this week. Let me know of your reading and viewing (movies, etc.) and activities. I miss you all too, but maybe these exchanges will bridge the gap. Let me hear from you. Arch"

[Then, after returning to Union City for the winter, he came back to his loft in the spring and wrote to me again.]

"Stockwood July 15, 1956
Dear Bid, With my belly full of a pork chop, baked beans and green peas and a can of beer, salad, coffee and chorag, [an imitation of the beginning of my own letter] I am all set to answer your very enjoyable letter telling me about yourself and doings.

"It is 7:30, I am listening to WQXR [on a little old Philco with scratchy reception] and I have just finished painting for the day. I am trying to gather my thoughts and get started and looking for an opening. Should I answer your comments or tell you about my own work. I guess the latter would be more interesting [to him] at the moment. Well, I got over that.

"My work has changed quite a lot since you saw me in May. I have succeeded in getting broader strokes and more contrast throughout the total. Since we should see things totally as possible I have been starting to compose in one big total pattern that is evident in every form and area so the full import is seen immediately.

"This is not easy since nature must be shown at the same time, and transposition must be made to get a pattern that is in color, yet contrasting in blacks and whites all over. Most of the time it is easy to fall into drawing nature as we see it, rather than maintaining a strict pattern.

"It is only by trial and error (hard work) that one learns about composing. It took Picasso ten years to get through his cubist phase and learn structure, after which he could come back to nature and his classical period.

"However it is the enjoyable duty of all artists who wish to do good work to go through this phase and try to understand what makes the wheels tick, so his purpose is welded to his mind and he can contain his emotions into an understandable pattern, rather than spill them into his work and not know where he is going.

"Knowledge and logic always win out. Emotion is a separate thing that you have or have not a lot of. It is your usage that counts. This is the craft each artist learns and it is a slow adding-to-daily process that makes for enjoyment and is our reward.

"Of course if we can get paid at the same time once in a while so much the better, but that is a separate matter to be shared by all of us and is just as important, as I have found it is hard to work on an empty stomach, if at all.

"I have done less work than last year, but it is of better quality...less rocks and trees and more figures, nudes, interiors...I am really encouraged, as some of the work has improved so vastly I am trying to hold on by working in all mediums in the same way, blacks and whites, watercolors, oils, etc.

"I started off rather realistically and then broadened the compositions by big black strokes. This changed the whole viewpoint and I sometimes found it difficult to complete some of the pictures; however this is the realm of good composition practiced by the masters who knew transposition into pattern in every stroke and edge.

"Now I am working on larger pictures and hope to be more conscious of strokes and edges and tones. Nature is not to be imitated but redone on the artist's own terms. If he doesn't know nature intimately he can never re-do it.

"All good writing also contains this pattern of action and movement, as I am sure you are finding out. I was conscious from the beginning of movement in everything, without which artistic life becomes static and dull. Every artist is only as good as his movement.

"In art the line is the strongest thing, and I have always tried to understand it along with movement, which is why my favorite men are Ingres, Degas, Matisse, and Picasso, as well as Cezanne, whose structure and use of forms were analogous to it.

"This of course is true with writers; the great ones have plenty of movement and leave some things to the imagination. I know you are conscious of these things, but truly understanding them is a matter of study, and the length of time you devote to it depends on you. Many artists never bother to understand this and after their success comes to an end of the road they fizzle out...

"I enjoyed your letters...and I hope your story will be improved by your continual work on it, but I also hope you do not lose some of your good points (as we all can in re-working.) Remember, action and thought must go together.

"However, it is ONLY by reworking with the changes that spoils the work that one learns. You can always start off again, losing nothing but a good time.

"I liked your comments on Faulkner and am glad you can finally read him...At least in your job you have time to read, which you may as well take advantage of. [I would not turn sixteen until August, and still too young for a regular job I worked part-time minding an office for a family friend who was a salesman.]

"...I have also been doing some reading: *View From Pompey's Head, Lion In The Morning, The Adventuress* by Haycox, and *Noble Savage* about Gauguin, which I liked....

"Take care of yourself and have happy times. Don't forget to write."

"Woodstock, August 24, 1956

Dear Bid, Just got your letter, which I enjoyed, as your

comments are interesting and searching. I am doing a lot of searching myself and sifting out old ideas from the new, by new of course I mean making old ones look fresh.

"Some friends just left and after the usual comments and criticisms about my work I am settling down to see for myself if I have done anything worthwhile. I am sure I have learned and improved lots, but am also pleased that I can drop a lot of it and do better work.

"The ability to drop is as important as absorbing; it is only by dropping, at my stage of the game, not yours, that I can get fresher viewpoints. You are in the absorbing stage. However, in all stages, there is the usual absorbing and dropping if one understands what art is about.

"You cannot drop something without filling or replacing the emptiness with something just as strong. Too many artists absorb too much at the beginning and then drop too much toward the end and never reach a balance.

"This balance depends on a knowledge of structure wherein each part reacts to another. I enjoy learning this, and it is only by living that one can understand it, experience it, and then relate to art, which then sends you back to life and all its diversities.

"The artist becomes as great as his contact with life and not his contact with his camera (his eyes.) I suppose you are realizing this with your short story. However we must accept what we have done today and let time give us a few more answers. Well, enough of this, I will get back to work and perhaps do better in my last few weeks here. Regards to your Ma and Tom and Elise [Tom's new wife.] I will be here into Sept., so keep writing me.

"Woodstock, June 13, 1957
Dear Bid, Just a postcard from the Woodstock front...have done painting #1 and it look a lot different from the one you saw.

"My place was insulated which accounts for my getting started late. Have also succeeded in starting The Model and The Mountain. I never thought I would, but it is now off to the usual Ernest H. beginning.

"It is quite different seeing things in print than in paint. Have also done some research for another book about conquistadors. Let me know what you are doing and if you are working on anything new. The weather here has been very hot but it passes into cool nights.

"Am going to exhibit some watercolors in a local gallery [Hubesch] and hope the tourist trade will buy a couple....

"On the Woodstock Scene 6/29/57

....In the meantime I am going ahead and producing more of my masterpieces, more watercolors but also more inks and charcoals, as well as a few oils. I am cutting down on the oils and concentrating on the drawing since there seems to be more a market for it than the oils, which everyone thinks they can do and are doing. Of course most of them are run-of-the-mill scenic stuff....

"....Nothing is not too unimportant that it cannot be learned and digested and made conscious; every detail must be conquered by itself and made part of the whole. It is only by thinking of everything relatively and not for itself that this can be reached....This is not as difficult as it sounds, but most people cannot do it....

"In the meantime I have finished my first chapter of The Model and The Mountain....I really enjoyed going back six years and recreating my first impressions of 'Stockwood'.... I also have drawings from when I first came, to which I can refer....

"You in turn will have to remember your own details by making notes, such as Maughm did in his notebooks....I am re-reading Hemingway, Maughm, C.S. Forester, and London. They all know how to tell a story, which is what we want to do. This is the stuff that will sell, good stuff....

"Give my best to your Ma. I'm really enjoying her chorag.

"July 11, 1957

...The word movement is probably the most important word you can think about, it is the life blood of art...

"I am sorry this has been so long a letter [most of it a repetition of his obsession with "nature" and "finding a pattern and totality"

but I have enjoyed getting my thoughts together on this matter.
"...Nature, or life, has the answers, and I will dig them out.
This is the pleasure of growth. I can't expect from art anything else
but the pleasure of working at it.
"...Work hard and have fun. Both never killed anyone.

"July 22, 1957
....Have a picture in the League exhibition here, which they
placed right above a Chavez painting. [A successful artist whose
work was selling.] Some people told me they like mine too. Some
say better. His is more abstract and they might not understand it.
However his abstractions lack excitement and movement, proof of
a good picture. Mine is a night scene, pleasing in color and with a
sense of drama and reality that I like to work for.
    "My new things are more violent and expressionistic, perhaps
in the tradition of Van Gogh and La Motte, modern but not abstract. Anyway, they have released me from the conception of a
few weeks ago. I seem to understand more of Picasso, Matisse, and
DeKooning's and Kline's and Pollack's motives....
    "Have not sold anything at the gallery yet. With all the work
being done it is something to sell a picture....

"Woodstock, June 17, 1958....
I was just reading *To Have And To Have Not* the other day, it is
quite powerful and stark and always seems alive. This brings me to
my work; it is also getting more stark and more alive, I hope.
    "I am succeeding in getting more and more away from the il-
lusion of nature, although I am still using its subject matter... You
can't be a phony cubist...you have to know nature and its ways to
be convincing in your own mind...There is no limit to how far this
can go and Picasso has been doing it for fifty years...
    "...There is no doubt the public knows something good when
it sees it, but there has to be a perfect set-up for them to recognize it. They are not interested in your struggles, would like to be,
but have their own troubles. Some artists resent this and become
bitter. Their bitterness closes their minds and they never better

their work.

"Regards to your Ma. Just finished her 'chaw-rag' a few days ago…. Tell Tom his imitation leopard skin is coming in handy these cold nights. However I prefer the cold to the heat, though one can move around more in the heat. The cold also drives the gnats away, which bite like hell.

"Have done a few more pages on my 'story,' but can't get too much out at one time; it always takes second place in my mind. It may take ten years to write. Maybe that's the way it's supposed to be.

"Hope I have not bored you too much, but these are things I have been thinking about and I am writing them down for my own good, as you know. Write again, I always enjoy your letters and a good bull session.

"July 9, 1958…

I told you I was trying to get rid of illustration in my work…I have been doing this subconsciously all these years thinking I could create a new kind of illustration, now I realize I must lose it altogether…. No one does illustration if they can do better…. I am thinking more spacially, more in line and bigger planes, everything more and more and less of natural appearances….

"I am going for little dips on hot days in the creek where you got some driftwood, and also some sketching there at the same time. Things are pretty slow up here. None of my New York friends are coming up anymore, though I have one couple who drop in every once in a while, to bull throw about their art. Perhaps this way I'll get more work done."

* * *

I would see him less after I went away to college, but I would continue to visit him whenever I could, both in the Catskills and in Union City, where his paintings would pile in the apartment he shared with his father and sister, as well as in their section of the basement.

Years later, after they moved to Long Island, he would store them in the dirt floor garage and continue piling more paintings on top of them, and most of those he refers to in his letters of the Fifties would become so rotten I would have to dump them into the black hole of the garbage truck, where their deliquescence would become part of the nature of his quest.

I do however have a little landscape on canvas-board before he had discovered Woodstock, dated and signed: "March 23, 1951, River Road, W.N.Y." [West New York] that he probably painted plein air down the cliff by the river across from Manhattan.

You can see how far from it he would reach by his last years. Fortunately I had it here before the others were taken from me by Little Aram.

And this theft would be part of human nature, whose story I try to weave with my own lines.

River Road, West New York, 1951 (Color altered in reproduction)

Art and Family

Attached with this chapter are seven family photos. Those from Coney Island must have been sometime in the early Thirties and the early ones in the Twenties.

Humans can't survive alone, least of all an artist, and like Van Gogh, Archie had a sibling, and she would pay the rent in Union City after he started going to Woodstock.

He was only sixteen when he had paid the rent for her and the rest of his family during the Depression, which he would continue to do until he was drafted, and then it was Armen's turn.

Yet she loved him and would never leave him, and they would live together for the rest of his life, except when he was in Woodstock.

And I loved her as much as I loved him, and how and why she would betray my love would be part of what my story is about, but this would come after he died.

She was a sweet and gentle woman whose terrible side wouldn't surface until her old age, though I first saw it one Sunday morning when I was a child and she had left her bedroom door open.

Then returning from the bathroom and seeing me fascinated by what was on her bed, she scolded me with an anger that froze me with the same fear I would always have with all my femme fatales.

"Stay out of here!" she said as I stood looking up at her. "I don't want you coming in here again."

Twenty years older than I and in her mid-twenties then, she was at the peak of her beauty while young men were returning from the war, and she would just be getting up from a Saturday night date when I would visit after praying for my father in the little church up the block.

She loved my father very deeply, and she had slept in the same room with him when she was a child herself, though I didn't know this until after Archie died and I had come back east to salvage his paintings.

"I remember," she would say, "how happy your father was

Armen, Armenag, & Archie

Archie, Armen, Armenag

when he held you up for me to see from the window."

It was when I was just baptized in the church and he had carried me to her apartment building and couldn't come up to the apartment because her father was still loyal to Annah's ban.

Yet she had always kept in touch with him despite the ban, she would later tell me, and she had visited my father in secret while he was living alone in a rented room during my mother's divorce.

He had been a second father to her, and she had loved my mother as well, who had sewn her a dress when she was a child that she would remember for the rest of her life, and she had also loved my brother who was her cousin on her father's side.

But I would never really know if she had any love for me or not, because I was too consumed with needing it, and all the women I would later fall in love with would be just like her, each of whom would get angry in the same way at my peeking into their secret bedrooms.

And that Sunday when she had frightened me may have been the same as when Archie read to me from *Prince Valiant* in the parlor by her room where her door was always closed while who knew what she was doing in there by herself?

Then lo and behold she had left it open to go to the bathroom, and there on the chenille of her bedspread were the magazine pictures of the movie starlets, Ava Gardner and Hedy Lamar and Rita Hayworth, as if they were her goddesses.

So that's what she was doing all those Sundays when her door was closed, she was looking in her mirror wanting to be beautiful in the same way, and I wanted to tell her: You are, you are! But she would never listen.

And when she was old and I wanted to photograph her for my mother who hadn't seen her in years, she got angry with me with that same anger that had frozen me with fear when I was a child.

In fact she had always hated to be photographed, and her vanity was really the other side of her shame, as if she were never good enough for the dream man who never appeared, which was partly why she never married, though dozens of men would have wanted her.

The other part was her at-

Zaroohe, Armen and Archie

Archie with diploma, age 16

tachment to her father and her brother, who had raised her when her mother was bedridden in the gloom of the Depression.

And so it was not true that she would not marry because they needed her; no, it was that she felt safe and secure in her secret

Archie circa 1930?

Hagop, Archie, ?, and Armenag,
Coney Island, circa 1934

room, and when she came out they would always be near, especially Archie whose humor and good nature was just like her mother's, whom she had loved so deeply and then lost so painfully when she was only a girl.

She herself however was just like her father, Hagop, though I wouldn't be able to see this until after he died and I would piece together my memories of him with my mother's description:

"A decent and honorable man who never hurt anyone, and yet so passive he lived his life as if sitting on eggs, afraid to move lest one would break."

I wouldn't get to really know him until I was a teen, since he had never spoken to me when I was a child, except once to scold me for peeking into the refrigerator like I had peeked into his daughter's room, though he said it without anger and only as a kind of rule.

"You don't look into other people's refrigerators," he said in Armenian.

And though his voice was as soft as always, it reminded me that I was to him not part of his family but only a guest.

And so I would keep my distance from him, until years later when we happened to be alone together for the first time.

It was in that same summer when Archie first wrote to me

from Woodstock, and I had come to visit Armen who happened to be out, so I sat and chatted with Hagop instead, though I never called him by his name since it would have been impolite, nor did I call him Uncle because he didn't feel like one, though he had been married to my father's sister.

He had just retired with a small Social Security pension from his job as a presser in a tailor shop, and though he was only in his

Archie, Tom, Armenag, and Armen (around age 14)

sixties, I was only fifteen, and I saw him as very old and frail because of how slowly he moved, as if somewhere inside him would break the eggs of my mother's description.

Yet as I sat beside him in the sunny kitchen, he suddenly came alive after I had kept my distance for so long, never to realize until a lifetime later that he himself had kept his own distance because of his own reserve.

And he must have been the same way with my father, with whom he had lived for twenty years and yet never spoke to again after my mother's divorce, so strong were the boundaries and loyalties of family life, as they had been through the ages.

But I didn't know any of this then, and finally curious about who he really was whom I had known for so long yet didn't know at all, I asked him about the old days when he first came to America, and suddenly coming alive with me for the first time, he talked happily of the free sandwich he could eat in a saloon for just a nickel with a glass of beer.

And I saw in my mind's eye a poor young immigrant just off the boat after his escape from becoming cannon fodder in the Turkish draft, facing the streets of the new world with only a nickel in his pocket, just like so many others before and after him.

Yes, he was a decent and honorable man, and I didn't really care if he was passive or not, and his daughter was just like him in how she lived her life, as if she too were sitting on a nest of eggs, none of which would ever hatch.

* * *

And so I return to that summer when I would visit her while Archie was away in Woodstock, and no longer afraid of her, I was in the blaze of my adolescent lust, while she was so sexy in just a pair of shorts and a flimsy blouse in the hot and humid heat.

She was also of course old enough to be my mother and more like an aunt than a cousin, but what boy ever lived who wouldn't lust for the forbidden peek of her cleavage and her naked thighs?

Looking back now, I imagine she must have been aware of my gaze, yet she would ignore it just as she had when she was fifteen herself and old lechers would gaze at her in the same way.

"They were always looking at me," she would tell me in her old age, and I would want to hear more and she would say nothing else.

"Men were always looking at me," she would say, but they were the opposite kind from the one of her dream in her secret room, and I would remember my own dream in my own secret room.

Yes, we were much alike, my cousin Armen and I, and her betrayal of my love would become one of the deepest shocks of my life, but this must wait for a later chapter, and I return to when she was like a favorite aunt whom I would visit while Archie was gone.

Then one day she talked passionately of a book she had plucked from Archie's pile, and she told me I too must read it.

It was an old Penguin copy from the Forties when the covers were illustrated, and I have it here beside me like a talisman as I write, the figure on the front cover a painting of a seaman with books in his arm and a ship in the background, as if he is about to sail on the voyage of his life.

Yes, it was *Martin Eden*, and it was my cousin Armen who led me to it, and it would send me on the voyage of my own life from where I would write to her and Archie until they died.

* * *

And so the Fifties passed while she paid the rent with her clerical job in Manhattan, and Hagop would contribute to the monthly budget with his small pension while Archie pinched his pennies with his savings from his Hopalong Cassidy comics.

In the meantime I graduated from high school and went away to Rutgers University, from where I would write to him, and he would reply with the long and rambling letters I would later edit.

"Woodstock, September 4, 1958 [The start of my freshman year]
Dear Bid, Glad you like the campus at Rutgers. Sounds like Woodstock with all the green and the river. I also cannot get WNYC on my little radio. [The other classical station in Manhattan.]

"It sounds like the army when one is newly inducted and

running around here and there, getting acquainted with new guys, places, routines.

"However I am sure it is not like we had it in the army days. You have more freedom and more activities, less discipline and more fun with guys of your choice as well as gals of your choice. Do you expect everything to happen at once? Simmer down and save your energy for the times you will need it.

"I found in the army that to go along with everything was the easiest part, and once I did that I started to enjoy it, since this left me with energy to do what I wanted. The guys who complained were always in trouble with their time taken away for good behavior.

"If you are different from others you will be appreciated only if you are able to get along with them. No one is mature. We are all learning each day and only the conceited do not learn. Thinking you know everything does not mean you know it, experiencing it makes it real and a part of you. Have fun, work hard, and you will enjoy it.

"My own work goes on. I have finally come to the conclusion that I have some talent, though there are always some doubts, and I am trying to work in the direction where I think it lies.

"I am starting to work in oils in the same direction as in the watercolors. When I did a watercolor it was a faster version that was more spontaneous and colorful and exciting. My oils gave off a studied heavy look. I was probably too serious in my painting, thinking it was a technique rather than a creative act.

"My interest in illustration and my admiration of Ben Stahl and the others may have fostered this idea, but I am over that and have drifted in my own boat out into the lake and thrown away the oars. There is no coming back. I must find my own way. If this sounds familiar it is because I am still looking.

"June 13, 1959
...All art is a mirror of itself, which sounds something like Malraux's *Voices Of Silence*. [Published in English a few years earlier.]

"....It is pretty hard to seize the present fleeting moment. We are always held back by something. The more I think about this the more I come to the conclusion that I am only seeking knowledge of what is good, though it is past, and when I know what it is I will have the present moment, but not until I really have it and can use it...I am more interested now in symbols and directions of movement as well as calligraphically concerned. There is no end to this...

"June 28, 1959

Dear Bid, It's a slow hot Sunday afternoon; have just finished a painting and am sitting down to write this eating a salami sandwich with a can of beer. Your letter is good because it takes me back to my younger days and wondering about college and what I missed....My college was the army which shook me out of my hammock and knocked me to the ground....

"Have arrived by now at 42 oils and watercolors, six are large ones, which I think are the better ones, but the quality is even and each picture looks different....

"The frame has a lot to do with the selection of what goes into a painting....and makes it exist as a world of its own....

"...I am always wondering if what I am doing is childish, but sometimes it looks right and we go on... When I think of Degas always being doubtful and the great Ingres crying after doing a portrait he didn't get right, who am I to worry....

"We cannot say anything about Charlie who is not searching for art nowadays but making money to keep himself and his family going. He is quite happy of course, which has nothing to do with art but is an individual matter, and he would be even happier with an art director's job since it would pay more.

"It seems poverty is considered a crime in this country, which is why we are so rich and the most powerful nation in the world, though it took poor people to fight for it....

"...When do you think you can come up? Do you think your buggy will hold up? [My '47 Chevy.]

"....My friend Paul Becker is trying to sell some of my last year's work, but selling art is a tough proposition, since the buyer must see his way clear to the reason for buying it. Most of the time it comes down to matching the curtains and the walls...Anyway, good luck to Becker, he is a brave man and a good friend trying....

[Becker, a lawyer and a Sunday painter whom he met in the League, would remain his closest friend until Becker's death just a year before his own.]

"Woodstock, July 9, 1959
....Becker came up last week and brought another roll of canvas, 6 yds., and at this rate I will need another roll before the summer is over. Have decided to produce as much as possible; who knows how good it may be, but it is more vertical and has more depth and expansion....

"Looking out the window I see a great tree and the movement of its leaves in the wind, just the way Van Gogh has in one of his cypress paintings. I never saw it that way before.

"I saw it as a tree, as in an illustration, but Van Gogh saw it as a powerful design and made it grow on canvas by his way of putting the paint down. That he could not draw in the conventional academic way accomplished this for him.

"I am trying to think in these terms and have learned a lot from Pablo, but I am trying to use the system in my own way. DeKooning understood this after fifteen years of his own kind of illustration. The same with Gorky of course, and of course with Pollack. When I look at Degas I find he did the same thing, and though it looks illustrative it is really abstract....

"I believe what Kerouac says about writing is pretty good. 'Just tell your story, don't make up a lot of wishful dreams and put them together.'....

"Woodstock, August 10, 1959
....did my 68th canvas, size 34 by 25, the largest size I am using, but when compared to the former ones of the same size, this one looks bigger. From this I infer that there is more rhythm and movement between the parts and also more objectivity....

"Art has only to do with art and like money its improper use eventually destroys the artist…

"I wish I could work more on my novel but this painting bug has got me by the gall bladders, so I am leaving it up to you to keep me in the know until I can catch up with you.

"Woodstock, August 31, 1959

…I wish you would read *On The Road* [Published three years earlier]….If I had the brains I should have produced something like it when I got back from Mexico, but I didn't think anything important happened to me except a few pictures, whereas Kerouac didn't do anything more than I, in fact I did more, but he was able to project it in terms of people and action with a robust language. [He had gone to Mexico in the summer of 1953, before settling in Woodstock.]

"It shows I didn't know much about literature as I do now, but I was more interested in painting then and still am…It seems Kerouac's adolescence came late as did mine, though I think he is not as mature even now. If he can mature he has a good chance of being great. He was expressing something I should have done years ago.

"I am thinking about maturity and am wondering if it is a separate thing and we must not lose our sense of adolescence if we are to produce active stuff. The word maturity has a finality I do not like and eventually I think we may find that maturity means only 'keeping an open mind and accepting things as they come.'

"…My coming back [to Union City] is indefinite now; there is a competition here and I would like to enter two paintings… though there is only one prize and I'm not known to the woman who gives it out. So far only some local residents have won it and young people like Sunshine and Cornelia. [Painters in their twenties who befriended him as a kind of uncle. He was forty-five by now.]

"In the meantime am going ahead on my 88th painting and will soon hope to bring home over a 100 lemons….

"Union City, October 5, 1959
....We went over to your brother's new abode in Ridgewood yesterday; Tom came and drove us there.... [My brother married four years earlier.]

"Charlie and his crew showed up late and we all had your mother's big guvaj dinner, which was great....[a casserole of vegetables and lamb with a tomato sauce.]

"...I got a phone call from my 'agent,' Al Buono, [another good friend] who quit his art director's job and started a pizza restaurant near Woodstock.... He submitted my paintings to the Woodstock Foundation for the annual competition....

"Have also submitted two paintings to the Emily Lowe competition here in New York....Also Charlie is going to make an appointment with The Society Of Illustrator's exhibition committee to look at my work....

"In the meantime I have gone ahead with more paintings and am getting stronger all the time....

"Also your mother is now a gambler. She won her factory's World Series Pool three times in a row, making a total of $12 in three games! She's enclosing $5 with this letter, in case you need it. It's hard to believe but picking the winning inning three times in a row is phenomenal [She lived in North Bergen now, but would visit them often, since they lived near her dress factory]....

"I will let you know if anything big breaks, but of course these are all million to one shots and they will probably fizzle. But the excitement of playing the game is great. As my father says, 'Somewhere along the line a tiny puncture will be made, and that will be the beginning.'....

"Woodstock, September 2, 1960
....Going at top rate, have done 28 paintings, mostly landscapes, bathers, also have given a gallery two paintings done last year. Doubt whether she will sell them but have to try. Bombshell might fall!

"....Have read all your books. You must read them yourself, especially Henry Miller....

"Woodstock, June 24, 1962

….Thanks for your poetry book, *Sound and Sense.* Came at the moment I was lamenting the fact I had forgotten it….

"Becker was up here last weekend….We had a good time, sketching and roaming the dead town. It will become alive next week…Don't forget to bring up some blankets and a sheet…

"Am negotiating with a new gallery, the other one has closed due to lack of funds. This one is run by a Florida woman and she already has 18 artists so she may not consider me….

"September 6, 1962

…More people have seen my work than in all the previous summers, however no one has bought any of it….The picture I had at the gallery was not liked by anyone at all. Another good sign that I am arriving at something strange and will continue to do just that. This week am starting a new roll of canvas and expect to go deeper into this new strangeness….

"…Sorry about Yates. Hope he pulls out of it in good shape. [Richard Yates, whom I befriended when I lived in the Village in the spring of 1960 after I had left Rutgers for a year. I had lost touch with him but had heard he was ill. Archie and I read his first novel, *Revolutionary Road,* as soon as it was published in 1961.]

"I met a Californian Armenian painter staying here with his family…He hopes to sell enough to take them to Europe. He liked my work a lot and was surprised I wasn't selling nor making any efforts in that direction. His own work sells like hotcakes and are the "dream" pictures of the villagers …but he doesn't understand the abstract movement of the Fifties and has remained a romantic realist. The American Artist printed an article on him two years ago, and as a result he sold everything he had.

"All this, I suppose, has led him to believe he has solved all his difficulties and perhaps for himself he has. Anyway, before he left he 'bought' one of my very small postage size (4x6") paintings, which I gave to him at his own price, seeing he wanted something for his collection, and while it isn't much it takes care of my electric bill…

"...The picture I had at the gallery has not been liked by anyone.... another good sign that I am arriving at something strange and I will continue to do just that. This week am starting a new roll of canvas and expect to go deeper into this new strangeness.

"...My most important accomplishment this summer was the reading of your books, Joyce the most, also Eliot, Yeats, etc.....

"It is the development of the larger qualities in ourselves that enable us to bring things together. Joyce seems to have understood this more than others...it is comparable to an artist's understanding and daring in the use of geometry of pattern and diversity that Pablo understood more than others while still incorporating the human figure, something I am trying to do....

"This is what I mean when I say I have become more complex in my patterns while the common opinion is that things should be more simplified. Simplification must come after complexity and not before. Simplicity I am finding is the end of art and I am trying for this not to happen.

"A great artist arrives at it in his 80's, a lesser one in his 50's and some even in their 40's or 30's. It is a fight between abstraction and realism that continually goes on and the more of each the better, the less of each the simpler, and the absence of each leads to academicism.

"I have felt this all these years without understanding it, but I have seen it develop under my hand. The only way to go through tradition," as Eliot says, "is to be historically concerned and you must earn it."

"It has been a good summer...

[Dangling from the draft I flew to Europe for a few months and he continued to write to me there.]

"Union City, November 23, 1962
....All is well here, have read your letters to your Ma.... Yesterday was Thanksgiving and we met at her apartment....

"We brought champagne, your brother wine, and Manooshag and Vahan whiskey. The fowl went down well, accompanied by the usual vegetables, sweets, et cetera....

"Charlie has submitted my work to Prentice-Hall and we are waiting for the President to decide....It would be for the cafeteria....The public relations man called me up for a statement and asked how I made a living and I told him:

"'You don't ask artists questions like that.'

"He later called Charlie and asked about my character and if I was a 'beatnik'....

"Union City, December 9, 1962
....Glad to read of your trip to Ireland and the fog stories....I know that feeling, during the war my furlough landed me on a Scottish farm where those same feelings began. They stayed with me and sometimes in my dull moments I think about them and of course paint them....

"My 'illustration' was bounced from the Society of Illustrator's, so was Charlie's. There were 3000 entries and only 350 admitted....

"Union City, December 19, 1962....
....Your Ma just left. Charlie just dropped by with my pictures from Prentice-Hall; they did not appeal to the President.... Needless to say I am going on painting.

"January 9, 1963
.... The latest show at the Whitney...showed me that my work is keeping up and I am happy about this. Some of my landscapes remind Charlie of Gorky who now has a show at the Modern and is getting some acknowledgement....

"When you go to the Louvre don't forget to go to the Jeu de Paume, which is next door and has the best of the Impressionists and Post-Impressionists. [Its collection is now in the Musee D'Orsay]....I am sure you will see all the masterpieces except for the Mona Lisa which is now in Washington...

"June 23, 1963
....My work goes on...I seem to be going in a realistic direction,

but of course I will break that when I get bored. While I think I have done everything I will have to do it all over again, only more daringly. Life seems to be a series of childhoods and to maintain them is our objective.

"Have just finished reading *Life of Eugene O'Neil*, a 950 pager. He turns out to be my kind of artist. I seem to have arrived at the same ideas as he did, yet his life was quite hectic and he did everything the opposite from me; but I don't think you 'have to eat the whole sheep to know what mutton is'....

"....I feel I am coming to something newer in my work; I seem to be obsessed enough with nature to keep re-doing it....I am away from the abstract, yet it is a strong pull that I don't want to break....

"July 11, 1964
....Bring my jug of turpentine and a pancake turner when you come up...."

Enamel on paper, April 25, 1994

Art and Society

He *had turned fifty* around the time I settled in London, and like a son drifting from a father in his own voyage through life, I became more involved with others as he grew more isolated.

And so in those days when long distance calls were very expensive, our letters became more important than ever in keeping in touch.

"Union City, Oct. 7, 1964
…What seems bad to you at this time is really good for the future, if you want to be an artist…. [My own letters are lost, and he must be replying to my self-doubt in regard to the novel I had started, which would eventually become *Voyages*.]

"….I got back [from Woodstock] via Charlie who came up with my sister and his daughter [Gwen]…. I had remained an extra week, which was good, because the next one turned out lousy. Also, was out of canvas and was painting 'balderdash' as you would say [about my writing]…and was thinking of newer and better things.

"Yet the summer was very successful and my last weeks the most of all. After that, limpness! But I have recovered now and will start again with the attack.

"I will not bore you with the 'selling' part of it, just as it bores me, and I will not do much about it, just enough. It is performance I am after….

"Your mother called yesterday and said she had sent in your driver's license renewal….[I intended to settle in London where I would get a permanent work permit in five years, but I would return every summer to visit her.]

"She seems fine and quite active, going here and there…Charlie is quite set on his agency job as they are paying him good money…. So all seems well here, but you and I are not supposed to be well. We are supposed to dig up life and find it all over again, strong and pithy, colorful or serene, that is our business, we are diggers, builders, destroyers, and this is supposed to be our happiness, digging. Of course we could give it up anytime if we wanted to, but do we?

"I am alone now, and the people I knew from the League are away from art. Becker is still interested but he is tied down.... As Ernest H. said, 'Let's throw away the oars and see what we can do on our own....'

* * *

In fact the great river of art had formed a tributary that would become a river of its own where painting was said to have died and painters like Archie would become an endangered specie.

This tributary actually began when I was a freshman at Rutgers where Allan Kaprow started the first of his Happenings. And Kaprow's student, Lucas Samaras, who would continue in his footsteps, had been the roommate of my friend Norm Fruchter, and Lucas shared common roots with Archie and me back in West New York.

In the meantime Kaprow's sculptor friend, George Segal, had started his mummy figures with leftover gauze from the *Johnson and Johnson* factory in New Brunswick, and their colleague, Roy Lichtenstein, who was teaching at Douglas, the sister college of Rutgers, was beginning his first Pop paintings using Ben-Day dots.

Then in my senior year, when I was living with my friend Robert Pinsky, Robert was the editor of our literary magazine, *Anthologist,*

Pete and Pinsky in Archie's illustration, ink

which had published essays and art by Kaprow and Samaras, and I asked Archie to illustrate one of the covers, hoping it would be noticed (see attached copy of his ink drawing of two faces which are supposed to be me and Pinsky.) But it was to no avail.

Then in London two years later, I had settled, thanks to Norm, in an apartment in Spitalfields that had been the former studio of Gerald Laing, who had moved to New York after Laing's Pop Art had become a commercial success.

(See Wikipedia for Laing and his place in the history of Pop Art.)

Ironically Archie, who had actually been a comic book pioneer, was now immersed in his version of action painting that Pop art was supplanting.

And so I return to his letters of this period.

* * *

"….Take care of yourself and write as often as possible and I will respond. I would like to get down to some writing myself, so perhaps with your interest I will get interested. In the meantime am reading anything that comes my way….

"December 4, 1964

….It is fun to enlarge the inner mind. It is amazing as I look back, to even the last five years, to realize that I did not know what I am conscious of now. I am very slow, I know, but since I refuse to do something about becoming fast, I go on the way I have.

"I seem to be waiting for things to come to me rather than going out after them, but they do keep coming and that is why I am going on…if realism has lasted all these centuries, so will abstraction for the next centuries, and I am now able to work in both directions at the same time….Things are getting easier and I am enjoying it more and looking forward to it more, and since the world will keep going 'round and round' we go with it….

"I am not seeing anyone these days and I go very seldom to New York. When I do it is to the Frick or the Met.

"…back in my mind is beginning the roots of my urge to write…I read and I read…but I am unable to drop what I am doing even momentarily. However your link with writing is keeping up my interest….I don't know why I have this urge, perhaps it is because all of us must have something else to think about or have a mirror to reflect what we are thinking about. To see all sides makes us happier and freer.

"….I am reading anything I can get my hands on, *Steppenwolf* now…a new life of Picasso by Penrose, to whom an artist friend introduced me a few years ago….

"December 8, l964...your Ma came over today and insisted I
write you that the second package she sent you has all you asked
for and you should return only the one with the tobacco because of
the tax, the other one has the rash medicine and the zachtar, good,
boondook, and chorag... [zachtar i.e. za'atar is crushed sesame
seeds; good and boondook are Tigranagersti slang for dried chick
peas and pumpkin seeds.] She will wait for your call on December
23, between 5 and 6. [Overseas calls were even more expensive
than domestic long distance.]

"January 17, 1965
     ...I consider my isolation a lucky thing, since I can develop
as I want to...I let myself develop freely after the war and I have
arrived at something I like better now than I would have had I become the illustrator I once thought I wanted to be...Illustration
is still around, but we don't see much of it. Photography is in the
main now.
     "...If you can't write about people, as you say, then write about
yourself, that's people. I'm sure others will be interested in you if
you make it worth their while. Remember, each trouble is a story in
itself, it is up to you to find the cause of it through your feelings....
The very reason you are there in London now is a story....Your
letters are reflections of what you will eventually write, though you
don't realize this yet....
     "...I ball myself out for not writing...painting is much faster in
getting rid of what's inside, but I will try to get down to writing in
the morning and painting in the afternoon, and reading in the evening in order to start again the next morning. It has been a long time
developing, but it seems I am going back to my beginning again.
     "Have borrowed from your bookshelf [at my mother's home]
Candide, Heidegger's *Introduction to Metaphysics*, Russell's *ABC
of Philosophy*, Pascal's *Pensees*, Iris Murdoch's *Sartre*, and Ford's
Parade's End. Will report on these later.
     "Enclosing something by Saroyan in the Sat Evening Post. I was
reading it to my father who was laughing his head off, since it took
him back to the old days....Lately he has become very perceptive in

his own way...my talks with him make him think more....

[His relationship with his father was analogous to that of Degas', though they were of course from a different class. They slept in the same little bedroom between the kitchen and the parlor, and while Archie worked on his paintings Hagop would putter in the kitchen, reading and smoking his pipe until Armen came home from work.]

"March 1, 1965

...I have started late in life and have less time than you....After twelve years of painting it seems to me now that I have really just started. I am finally doing very large paintings, 45x65, 45x50, and they are very powerful, though I am doing the same motifs. My knowledge has blossomed and my need at the present is to continue what I have been doing....

"....Saw the work of Kitaj...and my own work seems to parallel his....Am sure it will come out right eventually....Charlie was quite surprised at what I am doing now. I will try to exhibit some in Woodstock this summer. Have also some prospects of selling a few things to friends, but this always takes time. Am looking forward to my best summer yet and to making some new friends....

"March 22, 1965. Your Ma dictating this letter:

'....This weekend Khatun and I went to the hairdresser's for the marriage of her grandson. I made myself a nice dress in a new style and everyone liked it. It was a nice wedding at the Catholic church in West New York, but there was four inches of snow. We danced and drank and ate. The reception hall was in Bogota. Today I went to Richard and Alice's at three oclock and Alice read your last letter to me. I stayed with them and we ate the lachmajoon I made.... Sunday I made guvaj and took it to Manooshag's ....Tommy did my income tax....About you calling me, while it would be nice to hear your voice you would do better to save your money, your letters are enough and I enjoy them ....For Easter I am going to send you fifty dollars to buy anything you want for yourself....My sewing machine broke down and I bought a new one. I was sewing on it all afternoon and I enjoyed it....'

"October 26, 1965
....My own work goes on and I am getting technically better....I am sure if Gorky lived longer he would have gone back to
figures....
    "Sold a watercolor to a girl who came up to see me in Woodstock.
It was done last year at one of the times I went swimming. Never
thought anyone would buy it. It shows that the artist never knows
when he is making money or not. The idea is to produce!
    "It was one of my typical 'road' pictures, and on the wall under
the electric light it looked very alive. The girl was very nice to me,
bought food, took me to the theatre, so I made her a low price,
good for two rolls of canvas....
    "Am reading your issues of *Studies On The Left* [a radical journal of the New Left started by Norm and his friends]... Will report
later....
    "Am doing jury duty now...an arson case with a 22 year old
colored father of four...we couldn't convict him as there was a lack
of evidence...Next week an accident case...
    "An election coming up...a conservative and a liberal element
in the Republican parties...Buckley the man for the former...It
is crucial...since Goldwater was badly beaten there may be a new
tide by the end of the 60's. Whatever it is I will still be on my own
track, I hope....
    "Regards from my father. He got a kick out of your 'Jack was
right!' [Jack for Hagop; I don't know what I wrote in my own
letter.]
    "I have tried the new barbering method [cutting his own hair
with an electric clipper he got from a coupon] and it works well. [I
would cut his hair when I was around.] It is better not to wait until
the back gets full, then it gets more difficult....

"December 19, 1965
...Have not heard from my landlord in Woodstock. The day I
left in September his wife was much interested in buying a drawing

and a small painting I had done in the back of some apple trees, and we waited for a couple of hours for her husband to come home from the golf course, but he didn't show and I had to leave. So that's the way it is. If things don't go perfectly sales are not made...and all is forgotten....

"January 30, 1966
....your friend Norm Fruchter's article in *Studies On The Left* made good sense though I have not read the book he reviewed in it [Clancy Seigal's *Going Home.*] Am enclosing an item from The New Yorker concerning him...

"....The subway strike was quite an event. My sister had to walk to work, something I had been telling her to do for exercise, since it's less than a mile from the Port Authority to where she works...Charlie also had to walk to work [From his commuter bus at the Washington Bridge to his ad agency, Oglivy and Mather in midtown]....

"It is all over now for everyone, including Mr. Quill, [the union boss] who passed away yesterday.

"My own work goes on, nudes, landscapes, some abstract, some very real...I have certainly come a long way and will eventually come out on top, there is no doubt....

"In regard to your questions, [about my father re: my novel in progress] I can't say much about the past, the Twenties are blurry to me and the Thirties a period of struggle and slow poverty.... How you link them up to my uncle is your problem, but I am sure you will make something if you use your imagination.

"Think of a normal man, learned in his own tongue, interested in the theatre, a socializer in clubs and groups, single, interested in the arts, a good stable craftsman, a good dresser, and just about like we are or were.

"Against the background in which we lived there was struggling in work but enjoying pleasures, drinking, cafes, weekends, nights, hantesses [festivals], plays, closeness of immigrants and their dependence on each other, struggling to get ahead of each other up to ten years ago when they all moved out of the Dardanelles [West

Hoboken nickname for the Armenian neighborhood of cafes] to
the Ridgefield, Ridgewood, Tenafly areas, then all winding up
with closed minds, treadmills, big dinners, heavy spending around
Xmas, etc. etc. ....

"March 28, 1966
...Went with your Ma to the Social Security service and helped
her write her application. We got out by noon and came here....

"....I realize my work is counter to all the art movements going
on, but it is what I want to do....Painting itself is being overshad-
owed now by electronics, sculpture, tableaux, etc. ....

"....I am still reading the British poets in your college books
and they make me commune with nature a bit more each time....

"Woodstock, May 30, 1966
....Well, I have been up here for a week now...my place having
been painted...which makes it look quite trim and new. It appears
larger now. I hope this will affect the largeness of my work, which
has already begun with two paintings, one a typical Woodstockian
landscape, complete with lilac trees and dogwood, which are in
bloom and about to fade, plus the majestic mountain in the right-
hand upper corner against the blue sky. This for the trade. The other
is a reclining nude in a newer more abstract style with the body
recognizable.

"My departure from Union City with Becker was held up because of his family business, but we finally made it. Your mother
came over and had made about seventy-five pieces of chaw-rag,
which I have been nibbling and dunking and which will probably
last all summer.

"It was a nice winter and I accomplished a lot on the mental side
of painting and myself, but I really prefer the physical contact with
nature and the air, plein air, as the French call it. Things are very green
and the trees very sparse this time of year, and all is fresh looking.

"My father and the Duchess are fine. She says thanks for your
offering to buy her something from London, but she has everything. Between you and me, if you can think of something mild and

not too expensive...but don't think too hard.

"....there is a lot going on with all the protesting about the war....Things for me seemed to have turned inside out and I am trying to get oriented. All this Pop and comics...leaves me cold, and I am turning to warmer pastures.

"Anyway, I promise to keep my big mouth shut when you return and let you do the talking....

"....I saw Charlie once in a while and though he is still busy at the ad agency he is still interested in art and in seeing the shows in New York. But I didn't go over too often since it's getting too expensive....Did see the Turner show, which was great....

"November 8, 1966

...Sold much more than expected this summer, but things are pretty much the same otherwise. However, it will take care of next summer, when I am expecting bigger things. [His savings from Hopalong had long run out, and he had become even more frugal with what little he earned from his paintings in order to pay for Woodstock.]

"...Now that I have gone through a period of realism in the last four years I must make something of it or go on doing the same things and fall into mannerism.

"But realism is the key to our understanding and we should go through it....Have gone through a period of flat abstraction and am now bringing the two together. One does not interfere with the other.

"It is a matter of knowing where one begins and ends, of using nature and making it work....Isn't this what the masters have done? Why should I be different?....In fact this is what all art is about....

"I have been reading the same old books and am surprised at my newer understanding of them...As we become more mature we realize we can get what we want through our sensitivity to nature, or life, but we must know we want it.

"In the old days I just painted, now I am thinking about it. Perhaps this is what I was trying to tell you and your friend Pinsky that night. [I can't remember when this was.]

"February 4, 1967
....Your Ma was here with a form for me to fill for her....Last week she went with Manooshag to a church affair, which was the sixtieth anniversary of its beginning in Union City. The new priest is being sent to Canada to bring the Armenians together to stop the fighting. [re: the assasinations of Turkish diplomats by young Armenians]....

"She brought some liver for our dinner, which I hate, and she made me eat some saying it was 'ohk-ta-gar' [healthy].

"I am very happy with your taking up with films. [I was teaching film studies in adult education.] It is the medium of your generation and of the future...it will turn out to be your bread and butter ...let's hope it will be able to go toward painting more. Let's hope painting will go more toward painting as right now it is going toward science...

"I'm trying to stay out of the ferment I see around me...young artists are proclaiming the death of painting, and that is their right of course...But movement in art is not scientific, it is a passion for humanity and not a juggler's art as our young geniuses seem to think...

"May 26, 1967
...so far have done lots stomping on the floor to keep warm... the town is still dead as in the winter, yet is very beautiful at this time when one can see through all the trees to the vanishing point.

"It all looks different from summer; the creek is running clear with small whitecaps and the vegetation is starting to come in gradually with greens and purples and a stillness sets in and some nights the wind howls away.

"My electric blanket keeps me quite warm through the night. Have been getting up late until the sun breaks through to warm things up...Memorial Day coming up. Perhaps someone will drop by to say Hi. Your Ma made me some chorag to bring up...

"What's new from Pinsky and Fruchter? I think you are quite lucky in having a few good friends; that is all that is needed to keep on working...it is in fact most important...

"Charlie and Edna went to the West Indies for a week for their 25th anniversary...."

Art and Woodstock and Littleton

I*n the fall of 1967* I moved from London to California, and Archie wrote to me there both from Woodstock and Union City.

"Woodstock, September 20, 1967

....Didn't sell anything in Woodstock, though my work was exposed all summer and there were write-ups in the local news about me....

"However I am now known as a local artist, whereas heretofore I was non-existent. There is no doubt that in a few years things will continue to improve, as my work gets better and the work around me gets worse.

"There are five times more woman painters now than men.... Things are getting artistically boring up there, with a sameness that is deadening. People are buying $50 paintings and only pretty pictures at that. Until this is corrected, how I don't know, and they stress art again, as they once did, it will remain horrible to anyone seriously interested.

"My large nude was rejected and the only nude represented was done by one of the jurors who can do only a school nude. Charlie liked my nude very much, as it is large and competent and real, no sweetness. I will continue in this vein now that I am back. Charlie was flabbergasted at my total output and the caliber of my landscapes. My home jury, my sister and Jack, were pleasantly surprised.

"Union City, November 19, 1967

...the important matter is to keep working with the drive toward what we do not know....Don't judge yourself too much, as your self-involvement can prevent you from seeing things correctly...The part about your father was great, the beginning good, though the middle sags a bit. [The draft of my novel that I had sent him.]

"I enjoyed it very much, as did Little Aram, who ran through it in two hours. [Little Aram, of whom I will write in a later chapter, would occasionally visit him on Sundays after going to the church up the block.]

"I also like its mosaic quality....Forget all those established designations of what novels and characters are supposed to be.... Even if you do not say Melina's hair [my fictional mother figure] was a definite color, we will get it from her actions and thoughts if they are particular enough and your development is probing and vivid....Craft will come as you keep working....

"Things are pretty much the same here, I am going on with more nudes and landscapes, and there is no place to put them all, all the closets are filled and under the beds too. I should stop and take up a hobby, perhaps write, but what do I know about writing?...[Many of the paintings were also stored in a long hallway between the kitchen and bathroom in Union city, and also in their coal stall in the basement after the switch to central heating.]

"April 26, 1968
....Your Ma is resting from work, as you know, having almost earned her [Social Security] quota for the year....She says at least you have a dog knocking each day, she has no one, but she is glad you are happy. [The basset hound who would visit my cabin in Bolinas.]

"She went shopping with Khatun and then went to Rosie's house, 'Popo's' sister, whom she has not seen in some time. Then she came here, and now, around 8P.M. she will take the bus home....She saw the little painting your friend Bob Ohannesian is going to buy and liked it....She said I have improved much....[My mother, an illiterate peasant, had in fact an excellent eye.]

"Woodstock, May 24, 1968
....Arrived a week ago. Place was dusty and full of cat shit. Somehow they got in during the winter, rather than do it out in the cold. Cleaned the whole mess with *Top Job* and am now down to finishing up the last large nudes....

"....Your Ma made some chorag, which I am now enjoying....

"Weather here is good, rainy and warm. Things are still asleep but starting to move more slowly.

"Have brought no reading material except *Magister Ludi* and *Sun Rises*, [he would bring his old paperback of the Hemingway novel every summer as a kind of talisman] and I'll draw until my canvas arrives from Arthur Brown's Supplies. A strike of the United Parcel is holding it up....

"....Just came back from a cocktail opening of the show where I submitted three paintings....somehow I am always disappointed in seeing them with so many others. I always promise myself to do better.

"I guess this is the value of showing, you see yourself among others and can't seem to see anything good out of it. However the lack of good figure compositions is apparent. No ambitious canvasses. Just Sunday stuff. It is here I am trying to get away from the crowd. However it is hard to pass a jury with this and get shown. Last year my big nude was rejected....

"....Am happy to hear you have started to draw from nature.... As Picasso said, "It is necessary for the artist to be on good terms with nature."

[Thanks to my friend Marian Hjortsberg, who lent me her brush and ink, I began drawing for the first time, though fifteen years would pass before I actually became a painter. In the meantime, in that spring of 1968, I was in the first of my nervous breakdowns after a painful romance, and I must have written to him of the terrible loneliness I was suffering while living alone in an isolated cabin by the sea.]

"June 21, 1968

....Yes, we are all lonely, but that seems to be quite worldwide. I remember last year complaining about it to my sister, but now am getting reconciled that it is everyone's trouble no matter what age.

"My father is lonely, and you may laugh and say he's old, but no, he like all of us must go out to the park and find new friends, who are usually women who come up and ask if he has social security etc. and how much etc. He says he never answers.[Hagop was in his eighties by now.]

"Your Ma also has to go to friends' homes etc. So you and I should not kick, we have to make an effort to get friends. And when we get fed up with people we can retire into our own work....

"When I came out of the Army in '46 and up to '50 I was adrift and uneasy, neck aches, etc. Charlie was going great and I was out somehow and could not get started. When I decided to drop comics and go into painting I thought I was going to learn how to be a better illustrator...the ramifications of painting as a way of life were unknown to me and no one told me about them....

"As I look back I was pretty dumb. All I had was a great desire to be an artist and I went at it day and night, and as time passed I felt happier, though I did wonder what would happen when my money ran out.

"Yet I couldn't turn back....and for me this was the right choice and it made me more alive...as a person...fighting my own battles and matching my wits with the rest of them.

"But first I had to make my own rules. You must be conscious of the rules you battle with. Every artist makes his own and his work will be greater or smaller because of them. You can become an artist without them but not a conscious one....

"I found that my work is a reflection of what I want my life to be....and that the newness I was searching was an acceptance of life in its naked forms.

"All illusions are man-made, and my rebellion against them formed my art.... Your own choices will be reflected in your own work and then you will "get into art" which you say you haven't yet....

"[Date unknown due to damage, probably fall '68]
.... I showed at the Woodstock Assc. ...and sold a landscape...a typical 'river' one....I got $42.50 out of the $50 selling price.

"I heard that the woman who bought it was wondering who I was, was I a 'hippie,' was it a specific place, etc. She finally got some information from the Real Estate man who knew me and told her I was a 'good guy.' I'm wondering now if that disappointed her or not.

"I also showed four paintings in a group show with the new Gardner gallery up the mountain...and she sold one for $200. Of course she was so excited she wanted to give me a one-man in Sept., but I told her the time was bad, no one would be around, so we let it go until next year...Am still doing more of my 'Big Deep' paintings—up to thirty now.

"Now for the last 'happening': My friend, Ted Lavigna, 'The Shadow' was up to see me around August. [A friend from the League who used to be a private investigator, hence Archie's nickname for him.]

"He was working on selling land in nearby Pocono Hills. I haven't seen him for quite a while, and he asked me to come out to Colorado in the spring... so we will leave on November 15 for Chicago, where his brother lives, then we will head for Littleton, Colorado, 396 W. Peakview Ave.

"... I am interested now in its landscapes and perhaps contact with a gallery, of which there are many, Ted says. His wife draws for one.

"As to your own work, I like your monologue... I was thinking that if I had remained with writing I would have been able to write like that, but now I see that my experiences were different from yours and I made a switch to drawing for who knows why. But we are not far apart. My 'pebbles in a stream' are as real as yours.

"Regards from Armen and Jack. They will spend Thanksgiving with your Ma and Tom. He is back at photoengraving after being laid off for so long, and he is happy about it, but then if he wasn't he would never show it.

"Littleton, Colorado, December 31, 1968
...left for Chicago where I found time to visit the Institute ... arrived at Littleton the next day...trips in the mountains, making fast drawings, the weather cool at times, feeling the gigantic qualities like Ernest described in *For Whom*...also drawing from the back porch which commands a beautiful view of the mountains and its approaches, Littleton a combination mining-looking suburban town with wide open spaces...

"...have done three paintings already besides a pile of drawings and already forgot what Woodstock looks like...Have shown to several people, but no buyers yet...

"....Weather is great and am enjoying myself; they have lots of art books I have not seen, and am even copying paintings by El Greco between my own work. Am left to myself most of the time, have a nice big basement studio with bathroom which is perfect to work in. We also have a ping pong game once in a while to break things up as well as a television, a color for them and a black and white in my room, which I never use, time too important....the only thing that matters is my work and its growth....

"Cheyenne, Wyoming [no date]

On my way home...first stop from Denver...45 hours from there to N.Y....Got your letter and glad to hear you are still plugging along as we all are doing, taking the good in the midst of all the bad around us....

"I had a great three weeks, wound up with ten paintings and lots of drawings and watercolors, all of the terrain. I emptied my mind of Woodstock and started all over again with new characteristics, even worked in a slightly newer version of paint, drier and more jagged and less intense colors. Also more space, bigger distances. The last paintings were of huge red rocks that are part of the Mt range running down the state....

"I had lots of experiences in the high mountains, painting and seeing and admiring. That is all one can do and is the only compensation one can expect. Had good meals and the feeling of family life--actually as far as I am concerned and speaking for myself naturally, for an artist it is quite stifling, tiring, and too routiny with all the demands on one.

"A young man can handle it of course, since its compensations humanity-wise are great. But its demands must be met in a certain fashion to get its benefits and still function as a growing artist.

"Only a Renoir was able to reap all its benefits, and one must have his patience and genius and love to do it. Of course anything can be done, so we cannot rule it out. But as I see my fellow artists struggling with this format it is rough.

"Only by bringing your intellect into the home can it be done. Otherwise you are only part of the economy. I have learned a lot in these weeks and am more adamant of my own road in art. We must let our own nature chart the course.

"Glad you are struggling along, thinking, reading, working, etc. In a few years you will come to your own choices and they will mean something, as it happened to me--but it did take a longer time than I thought.

"Well, have a nice Xmas and my regards to your Ma when you call her. You will come out of all this stronger than ever, you will see. [re: the gloom of my nervous breakdown.] Take care.

"February 2, 1969

...Glad to hear you have finally settled into surroundings and situation more accessible to the production of some work. [I had moved to Berkeley where I was a mailman before switching to a part-time pickup route so I could finish my book.]

"What's new with you? Are you on something new or finishing up the old? Perhaps if you contact someone you could get some bearings on what direction you could go in etc. In this way you could prove to yourself what you should be writing. Reaction to what you are doing will give you some indication of finding what you want to do, even though you may not be sure now.

"Over the past seven or eight years I have proved to myself that I am most productive in landscape and more creative, take more chances and achieve more variety....

"In Colorado I came in contact with a different landscape than in Woodstock and tried to isolate its textures, boniness, and colors. Presently am working in colored inks and crayons to reduce things to shapes and flatten colors and line, similar to Melanie's and Tory's work. [Tom's children, who were six and seven by now.]

"It's a grand game and while we are scared, as you say, it's what I like to do and think I can do the best--in the end it will come out.

"I cannot enter your problems, as you will not permit it and as you will want to solve them in your own manner, which is the pleasure we seek as artists. [This refers to what I must have written about living on the edge while my peers were securing careers and starting families, as Charlie had done at their age.]

"I cannot speak now to anyone about art, as all my friends are off it and even with Charlie our talk has run out and there is not much more to say. We are all doing our own little 'work,' getting or not getting paid for it, and so it goes on.

"We must all build our own traditions, since there are no definite standards to keep up with. You as a younger and newer artist have a better chance of doing what is considered new than we old-timers, who have only what we passed through and is now on the shelf.

"If you do not speak now, you may eventually fall into our category and eventually of course this happens to everyone, which is why I am trying to free myself from some old habits and get some simplicity. Still it is hard to talk about this.

"We are all well here and wish you will take care of yourself. Am looking forward to Woodstock again and perhaps this year better things will happen...

"Take care. Happy working and let me hear.

"Woodstock, May 24, 1969
....Read Hesse's *Narcissus and Goldmund* and *Journey to the East*, Mailer's *Armies of the Night*, and Malraux's *Temptation of the West*. Liked them all....

"....Have matured this past winter, clearing up a lot of things that were presenting themselves as problems....Time has a way of putting them into focus and we see them relatively rather than as objects or problems to be solved...

"They're all part of a pattern and not things in themselves. And of course this is what art is about.

"What more can I say, since our communications have dwindled down to mere conventional utterances about what I am doing, which is always the same, and asking you what you are doing and finding out less and less, though I have enjoyed your letters.

"Of course there is not much need for them nowadays, since

we are both busy in our private orbits and can only wish that some day or at some time we will 'clock' together and shoot a little bull. But I am sure you have made great strides. Take care of yourself is my parting message. Let me hear.

[He must be referring to the change in my letters that reflected the crack-up I was going through in those years. In the meantime, the world around us was going through its own crack-up in regard to the war in Vietnam and the cultural revolutions both in the west and in China.]

"August 30, 1969
….It has so far been sort of a sad summer….While I had a one man show up the mountain at the Gardner Gallery, and my name and show were hollered over the radio and newspapers a week in advance and many people came and promised to come back, nothing has been sold yet.

"Rains every weekend have cut down visitors to a minimum and people will not spend more than $30 to $50 a picture. Of course there are always exceptions and every once in a while we hear of a good sale, which gives us all something to look forward to.

"My gallery wants to hold my work until October, as she expects a woman's convention to visit here then. All this is quite boring, I know, so it is best to forget this selling bit.

"The horrible part of it is that they want crappy work or innocuous sentimental sketches. It seems my work is not even understandable (imagine that!) and I am too far out.

"The galleries can't sell art since the public doesn't know what it is. Abstraction is dead and no gallery will show it. I am now trying to get my work to look like the crap that will sell and though I find this difficult I am determined to do it.

[More than twenty years have passed since his sister was paying the rent in Union City, but he did always feel the need to earn some money to make things easier for her. He even continued to try his hand at commercial fashion drawing, which I would see in my visits, though it was really a half-hearted attempt and he had no feeling for it.]

"I am simplifying my work and not trying to beat Picasso or Matisse or anybody. Just a plain picture of the subject will suffice. I am not lowering my standards—just looking at things simpler and fresher and more understandable.

"I feel I have come through the artistic mill and can now do anything I want. It does make things easier and I am sure it will work out. What I do on my own is of course my own business, and of no interest it seems to anyone else.

"It seems I am through with art temporarily until I find a demand for it and a reason for it. My inspiration is greater than ever now that I don't have to share it with anybody. It is all mine and I shall pursue it with all my power.

"I am more than ever studying the masters and storing up ideas that are constant in their work, as I am not interested, and probably never was in 'avant garde,' which seems dead now, nor in academicism....

"It seems taste has died and we are starting all over again to draw and write for the young and very young. At one time this was not so, but now we are at the bottom, or perhaps we can go lower, and talent is everybody's. Then again, maybe this was always so and I am just learning it. What do you think?....

"I have been reading your letters carefully and feeling you are going through the old mill too, but there is a door out of the mill, though we must take care of ourselves and look forward to seeing each other again....

"Woodstock is really in the news this year with the festival that was held about fifty miles south of us in White Lake. Woodstock turned it down but the company kept its name.

"April 24, 1970

...I'm glad you are feeling better. [I had fallen in love, though I didn't tell him this and wrote only in general terms.]

"...We may be thrown for a loss momentarily and set adrift, but we must philosophize ourselves back into our true orbit. Artists draw themselves out of it and writers naturally write themselves out…There is nothing else but this and the pleasure of seeing it through by surviving as long as one can….

"….The idea is to make money at what one wants to do and not to do what makes money. During the past five years, since you sent me the Courbet book, I have gone in the directions of 'what they buy,' because I had to learn what that was, and now that I can do it a little more closely I want to go back and do what I want to do.

"Again that large gap, except that perhaps this time I may do it better and get what I want, because of the realistic experiences I just went through. This gallery business makes a professional out of one without making him an artist, limiting him to painting 'what they buy.' This duality in my mind will fester until I am able to push through to what I want and until I can put it on the line no will ever see it.

"The public is more confused about art than ever before, they want a story, an illustration, then they are happy.

"I feel now I am closer to what I want and know more of what I want in terms of paint. During these past five years I have lost, or rather have not thought too much about the ideals I used to. Things were more serious to me before, and I see now I must get back to that state if I am to get what I want. This gallery thing is difficult to accept, and it is only for those who do not know what it is….

"July, 1970

….Have been painting happily here for two months. Suddenly I am thrust into a project that looks promising. My friend Al Buono's girlfriend [now Barbara Buono] works for a newspaper… and with her I attended the Woodstock Festival and did sketches in the mud while she took shots.

"Later I worked from the photos and came up with twenty or so sketches which astounded me, and when we showed them to the producer he was amazed and said he would like to show them in his publicity, etc. There will be another concert this weekend, which I hope to attend and expand on the work I already did….

Photo by Barbara Buono, 1970

[While writing this chapter on March 9, 2013, amid the hullaballoo of the recent media blitz about 'Pinajian,' I called Barbara Buono in Catskill and learned that yes, she took many photos which she gave to Archie, and though nothing came of the work he did for the Festival, he did sell a few paintings in her husband Al's restaurant in Saugerties near Woodstock. Everyone loved Archie, she said, including her children.]

"I am also exhibiting in Southampton at my friend Roland's hairdressing shop and also have a small show in Al's brother's restaurant. Nothing has been sold yet, but am going through a phase called 'exposure,' which Becker used to talk about in the old days. He is now out of the picture and other friends have taken over, as you can see. Business is bad here, all the painters are complaining as to the lack of sales, but of course this is country wide.

"We are both on the go—so let's go. Take care of yourself. Your health is your biggest asset. Let me hear.

[No letters passed between us during the following winter, though I did see him when I flew back east to visit my mother during Christmas time. His 'on the go' refers to Pantheon Books accepting my manuscript. I had titled it *The Last Armenian*, but my editor, Paula McGuire, talked me out of this, and rushing to find another title I called it *Voyages*, after Hart Crane's poem Voyages II.]

"May 5, 1971
….Leave for the northern shack in a few days. Have done some oils this winter but about seventy-five watercolors…a relief from… heavy pigments. In watercolors speed and fluidity are so synonymous that a finished product is achieved within fifteen or thirty minutes….

"However it is only after being well-experienced in composition and learning from mistakes that it is possible to blast a watercolor in one session and make no errors… you can't make corrections as in oils….

"In regard to your sketches, you are progressing very well…. [I had gone to a few life study sessions but had yet to discover 'the natural way to draw' that I would learn from Nicolaides.]

"However I would not worry about 'shading' or foreshortening, etc. I went through that and finally solved it by not worrying about it.

"It did hold me up of course, as without it I could not illustrate. So I had to go around it, as you will too, by continuing to draw in line and see shapes in space against each other as planes.

"This is composition and what you will learn is the art of picture-making—the teaching of 'modern art,' as opposed to illustration.

"Study your modern painters to find how they put shape over shape, color over color, to form a spacial composition rather that a photographic one….

"Color is a separate matter that will later come over these planes to make a total image without the shading business that is commonly thought to make volume. This is the message of 20th Century art and what the public cannot see, as they are not involved in producing art but only in 'seeing' it….

"Also look at drawings by Ingres and you will see how his line is the '*probité*,' as he says, 'and is everything but the hue.'

"….While my landscapes may look representational compared to Pollack or Hoffman, still they are the result of an understanding of planes and shapes and lines arranged in an abstract pattern….

"Forget color now, but if you can work in colored pencils or crayons it will be the same thing as paint or watercolor.

"Become a child again and see things simply and flatly, but with your good sense of proportion, as this is reality and a structural sense of nature, which is the craft of drawing and painting.

"…Looking forward to your epic [My first novel, *Voyages*, published in June, 1971.]

"….My Pa looks in the Times under 'New Books' each day to see if you are listed. I was surprised. So you see, he is still interested.

"Write me at the shack."

Acrylic on paper, Halloween, 1998 (Color altered in reproduction)

Art and History

In May of 1971, around the time of Archie's last letter in the previous chapter, I fell apart in one of the most severe of my breakdowns, once again ignited by another painful romance, though I never wrote or spoke to him about it.

Like my mother, he had done all the talking whenever I was with him, yet like my mother he too had always been a great talker, and since I always loved to listen my own need to talk went into my writing.

Yet in the more than ten years that I had lived so far from him and had seen him so rarely, my love for him, like my love for my father in which my breakdowns were so deeply rooted, had become itself strained to a breaking point.

I was on my way abroad and had stopped to visit my mother, and by chance he had to come down from Woodstock for some reason, and we met at the Museum of Modern Art that happened to be showing the sculptures of Degas, who had been one of my heroes since he first introduced him to me when I was a kid.

Choked by all the cigarettes and crying of my breakdown, I was in no shape to listen to him talk about art anymore, and as we stood by the beautiful horses and dancers I could barely see them in the blindness of my pain.

"Yeh, yeh," I kept saying as he pointed and commented, but all I wanted was to escape and find somewhere I could cry again.

And so we finished our tour, and walking outside into the suffocating summer heat, we stood for a moment to say goodbye before he would walk to the Port Authority Bus Terminal and I would stay in the city to meet a friend.

He was fifty-seven by now, the age my father died and I had stood in the funeral parlor feeling so frozen and confused I was unable to cry when approaching his corpse.

Who was the waxen mummy figure in the coffin of the gloomy and ugly funeral parlor? Who was the father for whom I had prayed all those years and would pray no more?

And my crying didn't come until the following year when my

brother was away in the Army and I was lying alone in the bedroom listening to my mother talk to old Bye-dzar, our neighbor from downstairs.

She was telling Bye-dzar that the old priest once said her son would come early to church every Sunday when sitting in his throne before starting the liturgy the priest would notice how I would look over the candles with a kind of urgency, as if I were praying from somewhere very deep inside me.

And as my mother was saying this in Armenian to old Bye-dzar, I saw myself as a character in a movie for whom I felt so sorry that all the crying I couldn't cry in the funeral parlor suddenly burst from inside me for myself, and I buried my face in my pillow so my mother and Bye-dzar wouldn't hear.

And coupled with this crying came the memory of when I was around five and my father was sitting on the couch in the kitchen while my mother was ignoring me as she stood by the sink, and I was so angry at her I rushed to kick my father in his shin as if not only to punish her because he was more important to her than I, but to tell him to get up and do something about it.

Get up! I wanted to shout. Be a man! Be a father, not a dumb cripple just sitting there with your hand in your crotch!

And the memory of seeing him wince with pain would fill me with guilt for the rest of my life.

Why does a son love a father? Why does he even need a father?

And so I stood with my cousin Archie that afternoon outside the Museum of Modern Art, feeling how far I had drifted from him yet not knowing why, and he touched my shoulder with love and said gently:

"Keep in touch, kid. You're all I have left now, you know?"

And I wanted to shout at him like I once kicked my father when my mother ignored me:

Don't say that! Don't need me to feel sorry for you! I need you to feel sorry for me! I need you to be a father, not a poor artist buried in your work like a cripple with his hand in his crotch!

Instead I nodded okay and touched his own shoulder to say goodbye before turning to walk the other way.

Then after walking a few steps, I looked back to see him one last time, and he was walking his old infantryman's walk through the mid-town crowd, his smallness so innocent and vulnerable under the monstrous skyscrapers while my love for him was as deep as ever.

I wouldn't see him again until three years later.

My father and my cousin Archie

Art and Property

I *should now say Part Two* before starting this chapter, because I have come to the turning point in how the wheel of history will shift to where Little Aram will eventually keep Archie's paintings from me.

Armen had been working for almost thirty years at a company that made Kaywoodie Pipes, and when it moved to Long Island because the rent in the city had grown too high, she had to move with it or she would lose her retirement.

Had this economic force not changed the direction of her life, as it has through history for each and everyone of us, she would have remained a renter for the rest of her life, in which case she would have had no estate to leave in a will, and Archie's paintings would have been buried with me to this very day instead of being sold to millionaires.

Kaywoodie's move was very hard for her at first, and waking at four in the morning to catch the train at Penn Station, she would not come home until bedtime, until a year or so would pass before she too would move to Long Island.

She had cousins on her father's side, the Semerjians, who had settled in the Hamptons back in the old days, and her cousin George, who had become quite prosperous by now, gave her some money to help with the down payment of a little bungalow she chose in the little town of Bellport.

She had been close to the Semerjians since her childhood, and Archie was even George's godfather; but she would eventually estrange herself from the Semerjians, until she became deranged in her old age.

The Semerjians were also close to the Najarians, since George's father's sister, whose name was Tumah, had married my uncle Garabed back in Diyarbekir. But after Garabed and his brother Boghos were executed, Tumah was saved by a Kurdish neighbor with whom she had children, so she stayed behind instead of escaping to America with her sister-in-law, the widow of Boghos, who was fleeing to Alexandria after buying her daughter Manooshag back from the Chechens.

And Manooshag, as you know by now, would be the mother of Little Aram.

Regarding the Semerjians, Archie may have been named Ashod after Ashod Semerjian, who was his godfather and who had been a soldier in the U.S Army in the First World War.

And it was Ashod Semerjian who had brought George's mother and my mother to America as mail order brides for George's father, along with a bride for himself.

And so the Semerjians and the Pinajians and the Najarians were all very close, and it was only natural that George would help Armen when she needed to move.

I don't know how she found the little town of Bellport, but she would tell me herself that she chose her little bungalow because of the middle class appearance of the neighborhood, instead of a much bigger home that would have been the same price but was she said "in the poor colored section" on the other side of the tracks.

Image was everything to her, and like she once spent her pay on dresses fit for a duchess, so would she now use what little she had for a little nest that made her feel she was "living in the country" like Charlie in Tenafly.

But she could barely pay the mortgage and the move was not easy. Archie in the meantime would have to sleep on a mattress couch in the small living room with nowhere to paint except outside if the weather permitted; yet as usual he kept his positive attitude and wouldn't let the move get him down.

* * *

"Union City, May 10, 1973 [Before the move.]
Dear Bid,...I'm very sorry for not having written you, but we are in hectic or sad moments now, as we get more embroiled in this relocation of ours.

"Our income is quite limited [i.e. Armen's income and Hagop's Social Security checks, since whatever he earned from his paintings went back into his painting] and this move means a lot of expenditures, with prices way out of our reach and everything doubled.

"We can go over our present limit a little but not much.... Your Ma made her move very fast, bought a house, etc. without a hitch....

[Due to the same economic forces that changed Armen's life, so too had my brother moved to Fresno in the beginning of the Seventies, and my mother, who had retired around then, had bought her own little home near his.]

"My sister is now a licensed driver, which she is happy about.... I for one am very happy about the move, as our present surroundings here have reached a limit; it will also be good for her, and the outdoors will seem like Woodstock in the winter. I am looking forward to the dunes, ocean, boats, lakes, etc....

"I always look up at your former window on Bergenline Avenue when I go to get our Sunday Times from Calori's Delicatessen [across the street from my childhood home]....

"I leave for Woodstock May 15 [for the last time] but will have to commute every week or so, as my sister goes looking for a house on the weekends and I will have to be with the old Governor.

"He is really old now, but he surprises me once in a while with his alertness and desire to go out with his cane. I know now what it is to get old and old etc. He is still active, but during this past winter I have done the cooking under his tutelage, and have even baked the cakes. But keep this quiet.

"My work goes on—getting more insights and trying to look young and sketchy, but once we are in a groove we cannot it seems get out of it without joining new ranks, and this make it unreal to my own desires and feelings. Yet I am doing the same things in newer ways and with newer understanding.

"It is between me and myself that I work now, oblivious of anything outside, except with a desire to see other work which is stimulating. I have at last made some new associations with young artists up in W. who like some of my work and I like theirs as well. I see where their interests lie, the extent of their knowledge, etc.

"But we are always alone and this makes us artists, as you said in your last letter….

"Remember, we will soon be further apart than we are now—extreme ends of the U.S., and these few words are the last connecting links. I will never break this link and hope you will not either, so let me hear. Regards to your Ma."

* * *

Now that my mother was in Fresno, I didn't go east until the autumn of 1974, when I stayed with my friend Bobby in Union City and drove from there to Bellport.

Hagop had died by now, and I noticed for the first time how much Armen had become like him. Despite her good health and limber body, she had never been physically active, and at sixty-four she carried herself as if she too were walking on eggs she was afraid to break, her hypochondria, rooted perhaps in watching her mother die when she was a child, gripping her now like an actual malady.

In the meantime Archie had moved into his father's bedroom that was next to hers, which brought them closer than ever before, their heads against the same wall when they slept at night.

"I never really knew my brother," she said to me. She had always taken him for granted and now noticed sides of him she had ignored.

I had witnessed their squabbles since I was a child, but they were always amusing after he made them humorous, and they had become like a married couple whose wheels fit together like the teeth of a clock.

He had become by now more than ever like a frugal monk who didn't want to let go of a penny that wasn't absolutely necessary, while she would spend whatever she could on her little nest that had replaced her passion for clothes.

Her small salary barely covered the mortgage, yet she wanted to drive to shopping centers whether she bought anything or not, and though this was the last thing he wanted he would sit beside her like a dutiful husband letting her enjoy one of the few pleasures she had left.

With her head barely above the steering wheel, she drove the huge '65 Oldsmobile that George had given to her as if it were a giant tortoise, while younger drivers beeped their horns and cursed her from behind to speed up, Archie in the meantime sitting beside her like a driving instructor.

And though he never learned to drive himself, she left it to him to deal with the mechanic when repairs were needed, since he was still a man in a man's world where she had never been alone.

The tiny bungalow had been built only as a summer retreat, but it had a large back yard bordered by woods, and he cultivated a garden with tomatoes and greens while she loved to stand by the back door and enjoy the clean air and the quiet.

The bay was only a mile down the road, and for exercise they walked to the library that had the latest art magazines for him and the health magazines for her. But she walked as slowly as her father, and he would have to slow his pace to stay with her like when they were kids, an older brother being patient with a little sister who was just learning how to put one step in front of another.

She puttered in her little nest while he painted in his room when he couldn't outside, and since it was only about ten feet square with two little windows to the east and south, he had to stand next to the bed and tack his canvas on a board leaning against the wall.

Archie and Armen

He considered remodeling the dirt-floor garage and installing windows, but it would cost more than she could afford, especially when she cared more about the bathroom and the kitchen; so he used the garage to store his work, and it grew full in no time.

I was saddened by how little space he had now, especially since he would never go to Woodstock again, but he shrugged it off as irrelevant.

Across the island de Kooning's new studio was as large as the bungalow and the garage and the yard altogether, yet what difference did it make?

Yes, he too would have like to work as large as deKooning, but so what? He was still the little kid my mother once saw scribbling snakes on a porcelain table top, happy in himself as only a child could be.

I stayed a few nights, sleeping on the mattress couch in the living room, and I wouldn't see them again for another two years.

* * *

"[Undated, winter, 1974, included with a Christmas card he sketched with colored pencils.]

Dear Bid....We have not yet bought our TV, but neither of us feel we are missing anything. Don't forget we have looked at TV since 1954 and have probably seen most of it, as most are repeats. [Soon after this letter, Mary Semerjian, George's sister, would find a used but still good color set, which Mary's husband would deliver, "despite Armen making a fuss about it cluttering the little living room," Mary would later tell me.]

"We have finally made our first contact with a new friend from this part of the country. It happened like this: several months ago I went to a local doctor, as I was feeling lousy, and he made me take GI series, blood tests, lumbar X-rays, and even a rectal exam. All tests came out negative, except I have a touch of arthritis in my lower pelvis. I suppose due to reading too much.

"However the rectal doctor turned out to be a specialist who charged $50, and I talked him into accepting a painting in exchange. We also had a long talk and he liked my sense of humor.

"So this past Sunday he, his wife and baby came over to look at my work and it turned out he liked most of it. Then we invited them to dinner and we now have friends in Patchogue. He is taking the painting for his home and also some watercolors to hang in his office. I hope he can spread the word about my work to his fellow M.D.'s and friends.

"Another bit of news, which I hope will make you happy, it did me. I look through the card files at the local library and lo and behold there was a card with your name and *Voyages* marked on it. I went to the shelves and there it was. I looked in the rear and saw it had been taken out as recently as August '74....

"May 7, 1975

...Thanks for your letter. Am writing this listening to WQXR with one ear at the same time. Relaxing time now.

"Today did two drawings until noon, ate a ham sandwich, went to the garage and painted a landscape until 2P.M. Relaxed a bit, then began to dig out all the dandelions that are dotting our green lawn. They are nice but not desirable on a lawn. Will re-seed lawn later after I have mowed it.

"Painted kitchen ceiling last week. The garden is now 15x25 instead of 10x15. It is a nice large area for two people and a black cat whom we now have, named 'Orion,' for the stars we were

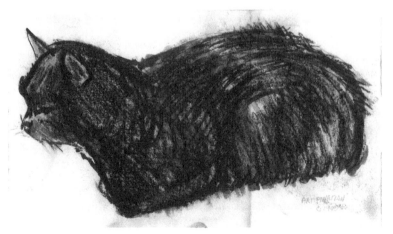

Orion, ink and charcoal

looking at one night, Jan. 4, to be exact, through Becker's 50 power telescope, when this black furry mass jumped into our laps on the front lawn as we bent down to look at the scope.

"I have fertilized the soil after turning it over a few weeks ago. We will plant many vegetables next week when warm weather is constant, and hope it will be more productive than last year. We still have squirrels who ate the corn last year, but hope Orion will scare them. He has been getting lots of practice these months and I have seen some near misses, but they are too fast for him.

"We enjoy his antics and ways. Have done many drawings of him. He has no tail, just a three inch stub. He is all black, thin, and very playful, and my sister is quite happy with him around.

"Later I intend to paint outdoors, behind the garage, as it is quite private there. Our doctor friend invited us for dinner. He selected one of my 1967 'House On The Lake' themes. Although I had taken a lot of watercolors he did not buy any, so my sister was disappointed. [He would lose touch with the doctor soon after.]

"I am feeling fine and keep busy doing new work and 'understanding' more of what I am doing. My figure work is improving as I am drawing more and more before painting in the afternoon. [Having no live models, he turned instead to Armen's Victoria Secret magazines and his old copies of Playboy and Penthouse.]

"Have a few more prospects but things move so slowly it is better to forget about them and just work. The dam will break later….

"My sister is well and rides to work with a carpool. I do a little cooking once in a while and we ride around each weekend shopping for food, Macy's, etc. I see no one except my neighbor. I will be laying down floor tile in the bathroom soon. [Armen would eventually hire someone to tile and remodel it entirely.] We have a new gas range and things are shaping up…."

* * *

He wouldn't write again until five years later, since phone calls had become much cheaper and I would call instead of sending letters. I visited again on my way to India in '76 and again on my return in '77, then again in the winters of '77 and '78 when I had a teaching job at Wayne State in Detroit.

In 1979 the editor of a small Armenian press, Jack Antreassian, wanted to reprint *Voyages*, which had been remaindered by Pantheon, and I asked Jack to let Archie illustrate the cover and Charlie the frontispiece.

It was a small affair of less than a thousand copies, but with his usual enthusiasm Archie made several illustrations, some of which took him back to his old comic days.

"Comics are in!" he said over the phone, and though I didn't take this seriously he was actually prescient, in regard to nowadays when comic book novels have become the new fad.

Antreassian, however, would reject his comics and choose instead a little scribble of two figures, one riding away and the other waving goodbye. My novel was partly about the narrator's father who was supposed to be the first figure escaping the massacre by ox and wagon, while the second was the grandmother who was left behind and killed. But the scribble was done so fast the ox looked like a "goat."

* * *

"October 19, 1979

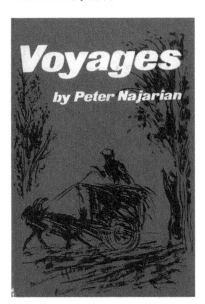

Dear Bid,...We wrapped up the 'Voyages' package a few weeks ago, and I just heard from Jack who told me it would be coming out this winter. Charlie did a kef scene, I was told. He saw Jack separately.

"I went in twice to see Jack and had lunches with Chuck [Charlie's nickname]. All in all it was very stimulating for me, since I made a 'big deal' out of it, to myself of course, and thought I was working in commercial art again.

"My efforts in that direction were looked down upon by Chuck, who said I was no illustrator but should do the thing my way, which of course I did.

Drawing for Voyages (Unused)

"I had done a fast scribble which Jack and Chuck liked; they had said to make it as indefinite as possible, and it was, but I had tried another more illustrative one, which Jack said was a compromise and Chuck didn't care for, though he said it wasn't too bad in spots. He also thought it should be a horse, but too late, the GOAT was selected.

"Going to N.Y. is very easy now, since in the morning I ride with my sister's carpool van. They let me off in Queens and I take the E train around 8:30. Got all day to look around and buy materials. For my return I get a senior citizen's rate, and my sister picks me up on her way home from Shirley, where she is taken by the van.

"Went to Parke Bernet Auction to see a large exhibition of Chinese paintings to be auctioned the next day.

"I have not heard from the AGBU [the parent organization of the small press, which also had a gallery]. According to Jack it takes time for them to make up a roster.

"I sent two small paintings to Roland [his friend from the League, a hairdresser who had moved to Florida] for the West Palm Beach yearly exhibit. It's a big show, so chances of getting in are slow. About 4000 entries and only 100 selected...."

* * *

No one commented on the cover of the reprint, and nothing came of the AGBU gallery or the Florida exhibit. He had turned

Charlie's Frontispiece for Voyages

sixty-five by now, but there wasn't any Social Security during his
carpet factory years, nor had he paid into it when he drew his comics. And so his sister paid the bills while he spent nothing except
for paint and canvas.

Mary Semerjian would later tell me that Armen complained of
Archie not earning some money during this period, and he did actually try to do greeting cards like his friend from the League, Betty
Ingersoll, who made her living with them; but his heart was not in
it, and the commercial talent of his youth was long gone.

Armen's complaint, however, came from her wish to spend as
much on her home as she once did on her clothes.

"She would really be lost without him," I would say to Mary. "He paid the bills when she was a kid and now it was her turn."

In the meantime I had found a teaching job at Scripps College in the isolated town of Claremont in southern California, and the nights were so lonely I had to drive over an hour to see friends in Malibu and Venice.

It was in Claremont I wrote my fourth novel. My second, which was published a few years earlier by a small press, was already buried and forgotten, and my third, which I had written in Detroit, would never be published.

I had passed forty by now, the age when Archie began living in Woodstock in the Fifties, but unlike him I was not happy in my work, and still suffering from my blues that had plagued me since puberty, I leaked in one of my letters the feeling of being unloved, even by him. He replied as always with the same voice that would sound like a guru's.

"April 10, 1982

Dear Bid,… It is Saturday afternoon, I just took a hot bath and have come out to write you while I am watching the Masters Gold Annual. I like to watch the landscape in color while the match is going on.

"For the past two weeks I have been working on a small landscape based on one of my Mexican watercolors done in 1953 when I was there for two months….

"This came up when Becker visited with his son and a Mexican lady who lives in Laredo, his new girlfriend. I could not put my hands on the Mexican watercolors so I showed them my newest work….They are going to Mexico City and she knew of some galleries and asked for some of my photos to show…. But I do not expect much from this.

"[Same letter. The next day] Just received a call from your Ma. 'HAPPY EASTER!'

"She is well and we went over the past a little, talked about expectations of your new opus, talked about Craig, Chuck, Tomo and the family, etc. As you may have heard Craig is on the verge of a divorce, Charlie is retiring next year to go on his own as an artist, Gwen will be chief pathologist at her hospital. I talked with her over the phone when Charlie called; she is interested in art so we have something to talk about.

"I know what a tough time you are going through and appreciate the things you write about in your letter. The only thing in it wrong is that we do not care about you. This is ridiculous and you know it. Everything is relative. You have as much strength and humor as we have, and faith in your work, too, and know too that your health will see you through. What else is there, all is for the Gods to bestow. We've all had our times, yours will come in your own time, age notwithstanding.

"We all go through gloomy thoughts about death, disease, our past, etc. The point is to live in the present and have only positive thoughts. It is these positive thoughts that push us on and keep us alive.

"I also cannot understand your ideas on change. The artist must develop his craft by pursuing his knowledge of life and applying it thereto. I don't think drastic changes are good. You lose something valuable and just for the sake of change it is not worth it.

"As I look back our change was a stroke of luck over which we had no control. We were thinking of moving out of the area, perhaps to Cliffside or Fairview, which I did not like, so when this LI area came up I liked it better. But we still have our present dilemma of maintaining the house with everything going up. It is the sign of the times. Again, something is going to come up to make another change in the future.

"In the meantime the only change I want is in my work, the change of understanding each day what I am doing, why, and how to get it down. In all my work I am always conscious of how I did it, what it means and my pleasurable pursuit of it....

"In my looking at the masters I have found that they never made a move without looking at the masters before them. I find my own work closest to Corot in its simple concept of solving a landscape....It is conceivable that I will be going back to the Chinese....

We go to the Patchogue library every three weeks and they have all the giant books on art...

"As to commercialism, I gave up fashion drawings because I realized I did not like and was not interested in clothes per se. [He had tried this during his early years at the League.] To keep up interest in fashions was ridiculous for me. I wanted to illustrate. I did not know what fine art was. I was brought up on commercial fare, Tarzan, westerns, mysteries, magazine illustrations, comics. So I began in comic books and thought I would go to illustrations, as it paid more. Then I went into watercolors and paintings to do a newer style of illustration. To my utter surprise and disillusionment I found I could not illustrate....

"American art lives on illustration. Now that Pop artists are passe and the illustrators have become valid as artists, it is all art. Art historians can't wait to get some present top-notch illustrator who can bring big money into the museums, on the assumption that their work is understood and bought by the masses.

"So the word ART is relegated into the past and everything becomes art based on the selling of it. And of course this is and was the truth of the Impressionists. They became the darlings of the rich within the past hundred years, as did Corot whose income in his sixties was so great he gave most of it to charity.

"The word commercial as we used it back then is no more, illustrators are now called fine artists...out west the good western artists who bring in big prices are some of these illustrators...

"Your emotion will sustain you in your work and it is only for you to transpose it into a form that is alive and appears new and is not boring to readers. Today's selling is made to women readers, written mostly by women. Updike left his Rabbit series, wrote about marriage and sex, became a 'master' overnight and now returned to Rabbit and just yesterday got the Pulitzer. I left him when I read the first Rabbit...

"You were born into a way of thinking and produced your work from that. If, after twenty or thirty years a new wave of artists think differently, either you begin to think like them or keep your own ways and adopt some of theirs while never relinquishing your own basic drive.

"Only the form has changed. When form changes simplici-
ties and parodies take over and only its own generation can understand it. Do you want me to give up painting nature and do what
DeKooning did by painting flat abstract painting, or Jasper Johns
who paints flatly paroding DeKooning by ignoring nature completely and placing objects into his painting? All this was done at
the beginning of the century...

[I never suggested this and his question was rhetorical.]

"Here now is something amusing: DeKooning, who is always
fooling around with reality, now comes out and says he admires
Norman Rockwell. He sent Rockwell a book of his work, and
Rockwell in turn sent him one of his own. Rockwell was considered one of the worst painters about five years years ago...now he's
considered an American master....

"Can DeKooning change? Of course not, he is the master
of push and pull and must remain distorted and on the edge of
reality....

"Degas said, 'I will remain in my own little corner and dig
away...I have not found my style, I would be bored if I did.'

"Why can't I change my work to make it successful as my con-
temps have done? Have things passed me by? Isn't this the theme
of Hawthorne's The Great Stone Face? I don't think so, as I see I
am doing some of the things the new boys are doing, while still
doing my own.

"Of course I am only talking in art terms, not knowing too
much about publicity, public relations, and ways of wooing the
public. They say now that the new so-called masters could not
have made it without the help of their dealers, and this could be
right. The dealers now will become the big wheels. The artist still
remains the worker, alas, which of course we are. If we think we can
write or paint something in a new way we should...We must not
look back, we must go ahead and try.

"I am doing western landscapes, using covered wagons and
mountain-scapes and looking at good photos of the west, Mexico,
etc. I am using old illustrations I have as references, and I use the

backgrounds and ignore the figures that were their first intent.

"Eventually I will get the feel of something that I am doing new or in a different way and thus will 'outgrow' some of my old habits. But I also am still interested in my own craft of drawing and composing, and by looking at the masters I am trying to improve my knowledge.

"Have you made any changes or tried something different in your latest? Perhaps we could keep talking about this. Is it more romantic? Narrative? New subject matter?

"I hope you will excuse me for all of the above stuff I have been raving about, it is also for me. I am sure there is nothing in it that is new, but I like to become conscious of my course and what I do next.

"Searching for forms is terrific therapy and makes me feel good and refreshed. No one notices it except the creator and of course sometimes not even he.

"The small painting which you picked as the best of my lot when you were here last, which I am looking at now, is a good example of form that will always be alive. When I read your Voyages every once in a while I feel good about it.

"My sister is now telling me that 'Biddo will never read all those pages.' I leave it to you…"

Oil and enamel on canvas board, 1988

Art and Breakdown

Eight years would pass before he would write again, since I would call every few weeks. Then one day he collapsed in a supermarket and was rushed to a hospital.

His heart had an "arrhythmia," he said over the phone, but he was okay. Like the war that had given him the G.I.Bill, what might have been a lethal blow had become a stroke of luck when the hospital social worker learned how poor he was and signed him up with SSI.

It came just in time, since Armen had just retired and her pension was not enough to cover their bills.

Relieved now of money worries, they settled into their frugal routine as the world around them sank into the greed and gluttony of the Eighties that grew worse each year, the rich in the Hamptons only a short drive away, including de Kooning, whose every touch turned to gold, despite his Alzheimer's.

A big change also occurred in my own life when I began painting for the first time in 1983. Then needing to see the Met with my new eyes, I flew back east the following year, and it was when I went to Bellport that my troubles with Armen began to surface for the first time.

Like my femme fatales, who all shared her personality, she had an antipathy for the kind of man I had turned out to be, though I wasn't aware of this then and still believed I was the child of her beloved uncle and that she knew how much I myself loved her; nor had I ever stopped needing her love, just as I did with my femme fatales.

But I had become a forty-four year old neurotic who annoyed her with my unhappiness, and she would become less tolerant of it as she aged.

I stayed only a couple of days, however, mostly with Archie who showed me his paintings, and when I left I cried on the train to Penn Station, as if I might never see them again.

I was crying a lot in this period of my life when my breakdowns were growing more frequent, and when I visited again three years later my nerves were so raw any stress would tear me apart.

I had gone abroad in 1987, not only for the museums but as if to flee my furies, and by the time I came to Bellport on my way back, I was so exhausted all I wanted was to rest with my cousins whose home had always been for me like my mother's, as if we were family.

I always remembered how warm I felt the first time I slept with them, which was around the same time as my epiphany in the Janis Gallery when I was so attached to Archie as a father figure.

It was a very cold Saturday night in one of those icy winters back east, and I watched as my beloved Armen tucked a sheet into the old couch in the little living room that smelled of the burning coal in the little potbelly stove and the linseed oil in Archie's paintings.

And then she tucked me under their extra quilt of the same raw wool that all Armenian families used in those days, and she even added Archie's old Army coat that Hagop had cut and sewn into a blanket, which was the same kind of coat that soldiers wore in the war film *Battleground* that was a kind of *Iliad* for me, and I fell asleep smelling it as if I were in the film as well.

What a treat it was to sleep in my cousins' home as if it were my home too, and whenever I slept with them again in the following years, I always enjoyed it as if it were a kind of Eden.

And it was this kind of Eden I was in need of in that summer of 1987 when I was so exhausted and took the train to Patchogue and then the taxi to Bellport.

Then lo and behold, the mattress and spring that had served as a couch in the living room was suddenly gone, and in its place was a new sofa too small for me to sleep on, so I would have to sleep on the floor!

Armen had bought it with the fifteen hundred dollars my friend Bobby had given Archie for three paintings, and it was I who had sent Bobby to buy them because he was making a lot of money and wanted to do Archie a good turn.

How could she not consider me enough to buy at least a convertible like Bobby's, who actually had the same kind of couch but with a foldout bed where I slept in his new apartment in Manhattan?

How could she not think of this like my femme fatales never

thought of me? How could she not love me who once tucked me in as if she were a kind of mother or at least a beloved aunt?

"Oh don't make a big deal of it!" she said with the same angry voice as when she once scolded me in my childhood for peeking in her secret bedroom.

I didn't want to make a big deal of it, especially since I had slept around the world in places only a tramp would endure, but her indifference remained an open wound that bled even more the following morning when I was covered with flea bites from the fleas in their rug that didn't bother them but was a torture to me since I was allergic to them.

And when with my complaining nature I started moaning about the flea bites as if I were blaming her, she grew even more angry, and the more angry she grew the more hurt I felt by her lack of love.

Why couldn't I just tolerate a few flea bites, she said, and I raised my voice like I once shouted at my mother when I was a child who kicked my father in the shin because she was ignoring me.

I always had a volatile nature and now more than ever when I was so exhausted from my trip and my nerves were so raw. In the meantime Armen in her old age was even more stressed from her hypochondria, and our back and forth became so painful I started crying again, which made her even more angry, as if my crying was blaming her, and her anger was the same as the passive-aggressive coldness of my femme fatales.

She had recently learned her blood pressure was high and our squabbles had become a threat that she needed to avoid at all cost, even if it meant never seeing me again.

"Let's go for a walk," said Archie, feeling caught in the middle not knowing what to do.

"I'm not good at things like this," he said as we walked down the road.

No, you're not, I wanted to say.

Then shocking me, he said:

"Maybe it's best if you don't visit for a while."

The shock of his words made me delirious.

Not visit? Not visit the two people who meant more to me

than anyone but my mother? How could he say such a thing?

But it was all he could say, he who would protect his sister as he had done since they were kids; it was his only solution to all conflicts, a withdrawal and a silence.

The day passed with a careful politeness, and I left that night, crying even deeper on the train to Penn Station.

* * *

I write this now more than a quarter of a century later, like an historian who can look back and see how a crack in a home will lead to a mound of dust after an earthquake, or what Buddhists call karma.

My love-anger for Armen was that kind of karma and crack, and it would lead years later to her signing the will of her estate to Little Aram that would in turn lead Archie's paintings to promoters and collectors, as if my wound were part of their destiny.

Back in the year following our blow-up, I visited again when I had to fly back east because of my Fulbright, and the blow-up was swept under the rug where our careful politeness would prevail from then on.

Six years would pass before I could visit again, since I was in Armenia for a year and then in Hawaii, though I would call every few weeks.

In the meantime, learning how to paint, I began to understand what Archie had been talking about since I was a kid, though ironically we had grown so far apart.

I was painting more than writing now, and though I didn't have his or Charlie's talent, I had my own, probably inherited from my mother, whose brother was also an artist, though it would take me the rest of my life to realize how to use it.

I couldn't draw from imagination but always needed an object to copy, and since I wasn't ready for plein air, I was limited to life studies and still-lifes, when unable to afford a model I had to depend on group sessions whose lighting was always poor.

It was out of this difficulty that I mailed Archie one of my studies, a twenty minute nude in acrylic on paper, and he mailed

back some advice.
I had listened to him talk about
art since I was a child, but it was
not until now that I began to understand what he really meant about
the difference between illustration
and fine art, though it would take
years for me to digest it, and by then
he would be dead.

The following is from a long letter I had to edit to make some sen-
tences read more clearly:

*Pete's life drawing of Archie
drawing, pencil, 1984*

"April 29, 1990
....Your painting looks like an early Cezanne. I like it, but of
course you have your own judgments. Your asking me to correct it
is useless, I would not know what to do or where to begin.

"What could I do? Everything is there. So I made a tracing over
it and put in only LINE instead of line with color. I have just gone
over what you have done and emphasized the line pattern of the figure, put in features and shaded areas before and behind the figure to
become a Total pattern.

"The idea is to create a total composition according to the flat
surface it is on, and NOT to draw a figure with realistic lights that you
see. You thus see a figure in its own environment. If your line pattern is
correct this is the painting. You have communicated existence.

"Line and color are separate matters—each is its own way of
communication. Your objective is to create form by using line as
planes, as you mention in your letter.

"It is not a matter of 'seeing' planes under light, 'artificial' or
'natural,' [regarding my complaint about the florescent lighting
in my life study sessions.] It is a matter of creating the look of the
planes in the figure by line alone, in its change in the line pattern of
the contours and muscles, etc....

"Space is created checkerboard style....

"Do not take my word for it, study drawings by Ingres, Matisse,

Pablo, Van Gogh....

"Once you learn what one did you can go to the next and see what he did to change the concept and make it fresher....

"You must free your mind from slavish copy and realize that you are creating an illusion of nature and not itself per se....

"You cannot do what you want to do, but to do what the flatness of your surface demands according to the means used.

"The drawing principle is always the basis, it never changes, but its arrangement as composition is presented as a newer checkerboard, like from Picasso to Mondrian, Van Gogh and Gauguin to Matisse, and Matisse to Picasso, etc. etc.

"The principle is always the same, it becomes a matter of leaving out and creating a newer checkerboard arrangement, Picasso to DeKooning to Pollack....

"Just as writing has been simplified up to the present, so has drawing and painting. Perhaps in your writing you need new 'arrangements'....

"'I am just a dauber singing my own little song': Corot.

"I am expecting that your intuition and feeling will see you thru, as I have by working step by step and enjoying it. Creating form by line alone is your next objective.

"I am still doing what I have been telling you.... I am tracing silhouettes of models in catalogs and doing landscapes by using line and daubing with *Bounty* paper towels....

"Be satisfied with good pattern, which if done correctly, is ART itself....

"Try to see everything as drawing, from cartoons to illustrations to paintings to photographs. They are the same, lines or edged....

"If you look at Matisse and Picasso...you will realize that both gave up Nature for the freedom of creating forms in space....

"I learned this in the Fifties when I went 'outdoors' in the summer and continued in the winter working from memory. I am conscious of this only now, then it was a fight for freedom.... I am still at it now, as the battle never ends and is continually changing....

"Am enclosing an old Armenian calendar of paintings that are great and illustrate what I am talking about. [By Mardiros Sarian, whose studio I had visited in Yerevan.]

Horse, Ink, 1988

* * *

Aside from my phone calls, I would continue to write to him about my development, always hoping he would reply with more of his words, and he finally did two years later:

"Bellport, April 4, 1992
....I am still doing two or three compositions a week and learning what to do and why I should do it.

"I am trying wildlife paintings, which if done right could find a publisher. But they want realism and good animal drawings and authentic habitats. You've got to be part zoologist and photographer. All this is out of my line, but I am trying to create some landscape-type which will fill the bill.

"My interest has been in art all these years and now drawing in itself is keeping the interest up. The wildlife environmental and nature bit is big now and everything points to it getting bigger. It is an outgrowth of illustration going west....

"There are many galleries out west, Arizona, Michigan, Texas, etc.

where I may be able to show landscapes if I could develop more realistic work. But it is too abstract…though I am trying some horses….

[Through Charlie, he had made friends with a former art director, Sal Giglio, who had moved to Santa Fe where Giglio would later start a gallery, and after visiting back east around the time of this letter Giglio had bought one of Archie's seascapes 'for a hundred dollars,' and Archie would keep hoping this would lead to more; but it never would.]

"The important thing in art is to understand what it is and how it works and then create your own brand.

"To understand the TOTALITY of art is to arrive at its creation. It has nothing to do with being abstract or realistic per se. It has to do with its TOTALITY as expression, the judgment of which depends on your own feelings…on a flat surface….

"This also requires knowledge and wisdom as TIME moves on. If you are conscious of TOTALITY, time will coalesce everything into one.

"It should. But we must keep our eyes 'on the ball.' Only when you know what art is can you do this.

"You are on the tightrope and the object is not to fall off… if you do you see 'things', 'specifics', 'details,'…the TOTALITY is not there, rhythms, harmonies, contrasts, are not there, all because you have not created them.

"When we do something good it is by intuition or 'accident.' We try to figure it out. So we do another one and another one. We repeat ourselves until we are able to keep moving on that tightrope by not imitating our good work but keeping our eye on the ball, which is art.

"Art is being created every day by someone because they dare to work. Not knowing what we are doing is the reason we work.

"I am glad you are writing about art. Writing about art is NOW an art form. There is a show on it at the Louvre. The condition of the art market has created something here I am trying to 'figure out' as usual.

"Degas told journalists: 'No matter how much you write about art you are not advancing the knowledge of the public a bit.'

"It would be interesting to find out if this new art form will succeed in teaching the public HOW to look at pictures, judge them, prefer them, etc... or is this an educational gimmick per se? It could relate to Van Gogh's letters, which were as much about art as his work.

"It also seems that your doing art and writing about art will coalesce, or could in time.

"Last time you were here you asked if you could do both. It seems you can and maybe will by writing about it.

"I have read Updike's book on his art selection, but was not impressed. Also Joyce C. Oates has writtten a few magazine shorts on Bellows' paintings and others, and I was not impressed. Perhaps I missed something. Maybe I expected more. Updike dabbled in cartoons. I don't know what Oates did in art.

"First writer I knew who wrote about art was Maughm. He wrote on El Greco and Spanish art. He later amassed a collection of Matisse, Picasso, Renoir, etc.

"Back to you: congrats on the award--you are now an Armenian writer. [I received the Anahid Literary Award at the Armenian Studies Program in Columbia University.]

"I am sure you will also wind up an American writer--Time will see to that.

"This coming weekend we will go to Charlie's for his 50th anniversary. Will report on that later. Will also see Chuck's new work to see if he is keeping up creatively. He says now that he's retired he's not illustrating but 'painting.'

"The fine line between illustration and painting has to be learned....Each is a version of the same thing. Rockwell comes out as an illustrator, Wyeth as a painter. Can you figure this out?....

"...I went into fine art as opposed to illustration. For the last ten years I have backtracked to doing realistic illustration which I am trying now. It may be this realistic phase will lead to better fine art, since this is what we want. But great fine art can now be realistic and/or abstract, as has been shown in this century.

"To understand art more than anything else has been my motivation in painting and drawing. Things are clearer for me now, but back then there was nothing but work to find things out....

"When Chuck called my work abstract I was surprised and not happy, as I wanted to think I was not abstract or all that abstract. As I understand things now and from what I've read, the older the artist gets the more he stays in his own backyard and develops that.

"In the meantime he gets left behind as younger artists come up with work a shadow of what he was doing with a fresher and faster look. But it does not diminish him—he stands out like a monument to be looked at and studied.

"Picasso, a monument, said: 'What saves me is that every day I do worse.'

"Artists have always said, 'I paint to get better.'

"Better or worse, the Lady or the Tiger. Is this a slap at the academic? His work at ninety was as 'bad' as it always had been.

"Enough of this—back to work—and take care—keep your eye on the ball. 'The Prof.'

* * *

After painting for ten years, I discovered plein air, and when I wrote to Archie about this and he replied:

"December 21, 1993
…Hope you are well and busy.

My own efforts presently are about line and usage in creating composition. Ingres said, 'You must do everything in line except the hue.'

"So I am drawing more than painting.

"As I look at paintings now I see them as drawings in line and shape and how they make a total pattern.

"I never saw things that way.

"I just painted thinking I had to draw realistically. It was only a step to lead to another step and eventually on and on.

"If you had enough outdoor landscaping, come indoors and paint from your imagination. You may be surprised. [I had mentioned my lack of imagination.] The change will make you aware, as it did Matisse and Picasso, that within basic shapes Patterns are created with lines and later with colors.

"Take care."

Art and The Wake

Back in 1987, on the same trip as when I had the blow-up with Armen, I also visited Charlie and Edna in Tenafly, and Edna, who had been stricken years earlier with Parkinson's, was now in a wheelchair.

"It finally got to him," Archie had said about Charlie in regard to her, which was to say bad luck.

She and Charlie had some good years after his retirement, and he had looked forward to painting in his new studio that looked out to the woods in his back yard, but then Edna grew worse until he had to care for her like a nurse's aide, and by the time I visited she was unable to talk except in a moan that only he could understand.

She had been a very friendly woman with a great smile and a big heart, and even after I was middle-aged, she would still think of me as the little baby my mother and father had brought to her wedding.

Now her lips were twisted even worse than my father's had been, and as she tried to smile her face was so contorted I had to look away from the pain I felt.

Behind her was the portrait Charlie had painted in Washington when she was a beautiful young Swedish woman with golden hair and blue eyes, and he had caught her liveliness at the height of his talent with his fresh strokes as nimble as the masters.

"Alla prima," he would always say with pride whenever I looked at it.

He did have a great talent, as Archie would often say about him, and it was true that in his youth he really could "paint like his hero, Sargent." But as the years passed his

Charlie's Edna, Alla Prima"
[Photo by Gwen in her home]

talent weakened like that of an athlete or a singer, and after decades in the ad agency, he couldn't revive it.

"I can't do that anymore," he said, as we looked at one of his early watercolors that had won a national prize.

His talent lay in his hands and his eyes, but something else lay undeveloped; what was it?

Years earlier I had bought one of Archie's Woodstock paintings when I was teaching in Detroit, and I would compare it to the beautiful watercolor Charlie had given my mother from his early years when he was at the top of his form.

What was the difference between them? To this day I am still trying to learn it.

Looking at what Charlie had been painting in his retirement, I noticed how conventional it seemed, though his craft was still clear. He was doing portraits on commission, and they looked like all other portraits that hung in official places all over the world.

His landscapes too were like those in commercial galleries, but the elan of his youth had passed, and he had not replaced it with what Archie had been developing in the meantime.

Instead he had raised a family and sent his kids to college, and now that they were gone he was changing the diapers of his beloved wife like a nurse's aide.

Yet like Archie, his spirit never flagged, and he never lost his sunny nature and bonhomie.

The fiftieth anniversary that Archie would mention in his letter would also be a renewal of his wedding vow with a parson and a ceremony, and I would cry when I received the photo of him smiling beside her twisted figure in the wheelchair as if to say he loved her as deeply as ever.

After she died he would visit his daughter Gwen in Sacramento at Christmas time, and then he would take the train to Berkeley, and I would meet him at the station and drive to San Francisco where we'd go to the Legion of Honor or the old De Young or the old Modern.

It was then I would really get to know him, and as we walked through the galleries he would point to what I wouldn't have noticed by myself.

"Look!" he would say when we once caught a traveling show at the Legion. "It's an Adolph Menzel," who I had never heard of. "Degas loved Menzel's work."

It was around this time I first learned he had been friends with Franz Kline and Jacob Lawrence when they were colleagues at Pratt, who were two of my favorite artists.

Lawrence had never taught before and he said, "Charlie, I don't know what to say."

"I told him," Charlie said, "'Just be yourself.'"

* * *

"Charlie really has a good eye," I had said to Archie over the phone.

"Of course," Archie said, "you just discovered this?"

I flew back east again in 1995, and when I met Charlie in the Met he said:

"I come here like going to church."

He would go to Manhattan almost every week to meet his old illustrator friends and see the current exhibit, and then they'd go for lunch at the Society of Illustrators where one of his war drawings still hung on the wall.

I went with him myself that year, confronting once again the old difference between illustration and fine art that I'd been hearing from Archie since I was a child.

Then I took the train to Patchogue and got a cab to Bellport because Armen's car, which had become an old Nissan, was not working for some reason.

I hadn't visited in six years, and when Archie came out to the driveway he said with his thick New York accent like the comedian Art Carney:

"Hey, Jackson, you here again?"

He used to call his father Jackson, playing on the translation of Hagop into Jack and the Jackson character on the Jack Benny radio show they used to listen to every Sunday night at 7 P.M. with their evening meal.

Armen and I had come to a kind of peace, and after we lay the cushions on the floor the fleas didn't bite for some reason, perhaps because it was still winter.

The next day Archie and I walked to the bay where we saw a flock of swans fly over the waves and settle on the beach, and I looked at him watching them with his sharp sight that were as clear as ever, though he had started to use reading glasses for the first time.

What was it like to see through his eyes, my Archie whom I loved so deeply?

On our way back we passed a little co-op gallery of local artists whose work he called "the usual commercial fare."

He had come across a cheap camera somewhere and sent slides of his work with a simple vita to send to galleries, but they were poor slides and he never hired a photographer for better ones.

He had passed eighty, and he said in regard to what was more important than galleries:

"I just want another ten years. I feel I'm just beginning."

"Archie," I said, "you said that ten years ago."

We were walking past a row of forsythia that were beginning to bloom with their beautiful yellow, and he said:

"My friend Becker died. He was my friend for fifty years."

Back at the bungalow I asked to see his early work from Woodstock that was in the garage, and he had to pull it from under a pile that had been stacked by the rafters.

One of the landscapes had a hole in its corner, and in the hole was a little nest that a wren or a finch had woven from the threads of the canvas where the sky was supposed to be, and I was about to pull it away when he said:

"No, leave it there, I like it. I couldn't get that spot right and now it works. You see: time solves everything."

"Archie," I said, "what's going to happen to all this work when you're gone."

"I'm leaving it all to you," he said, by which he meant Armen wouldn't be able to deal with it.

As we sat in the living room I tried to sketch a portrait of him in pencil as he was dozing, but I wasn't as good as I am now, and I

Pete's pencil drawing of Archie dozing, 1994

couldn't get it right. "It's all right," he said. "Don't fiddle with it. Do another one some other time."

He was doing at least a painting a day now, as well as drawing and sketching, and his little room was the size of a monk's cell like those in San Marco where Fra Angelico had painted his angels, and he was still that child who once scribbled snakes on a porcelain table top his mother would wipe away.

Sometimes he would stretch the canvasses, but he would roll most of them or collect them in stacks with those on paper or Masonite, and the recent piles were stacked in his room with his magazines and clothes.

The little cell of a room was so stuffed by now it was impossible to clean, like Degas' attic where his housekeeper was forbidden to enter or she would disturb the dust of his pastels.

Photo by Pete, 1994, with the recent painting Archie thought one of his best. A mole developed on his right temple in his old age.

His sister complained when his pictures spilled into the living room, but she really loved them, and since they rarely had visitors it didn't really matter.

Once again I cried on the train back to Penn Station, as if I would never see him again, and this time it would be true.

* * *

His last letter would come a few years later. I had sent him copies of my illustrations for my new book, *The Great American Loneliness*, and I had asked for comments and advice:

"Bellport, July 1, 1998....
Rec'd your package and devoured contents.

"I see your concern for better work. It's all our concern and everyday I try to improve my use of the knowledge acquired from working....

"In regard to your 'illustrations,' they all need clarification of detail and subject matter, texture, atmosphere, line separation, then perhaps you will like them more....

"Whatever you do must be done looking fresh....

"Do the subject matter in a composition of just lines or dots and dashes, big shapes and small shapes, atmospheric or real, etc....

"You must create your own style. It is the style that counts, which is a metaphor for the subject....

"Regarding my own work: I am still doing my own type of landscapes in different ways and mediums, with acrylic, pen and ink, pencil, etc., on poster board, 11x14.

"Also am doing a lot of sketching and doodling at random, just to keep drawing in line. Color I get in acrylics, which I like, as it is a cross between oil and watercolor, and it is fast. It dries immediately and you go over it with colors and/or ink line or pencil.

[He had preferred oils, but after sixty years his sister complained because the odor began to affect her.]

"I do one a day and it's instructive to watch the differences and likenesses or repetitions.

"I don't think about what I am doing, because I've done them

Acrylic on paper, 1995

already and it is their newness I want, the so-called modern look and colorful.

"I am also doing figures, mostly nudes and horses in land-scapes, everything organized into a totality. My idea is that a total-ity or pattern making an illusion is the expression created. All in terms of flat colored areas or lines a la Matisse.

[I was still struggling with anatomy and he commented on my admiration for academic talent.]

"The kind of drawing you admire I bypassed as I became a modern by studying the works of the American artists, Marin, DeMuth, Prendergast, Pollack, and also the British impressionists and Pop artists, etc.

"But I have kept away from abstract color field painters be-cause I like landscapes and drawing objects and figures.

"Each day I look at art back to the renaissance and the primi-tive to trigger my imagination and memory.

"The totality of art coalesces into a pattern of sameness and differences in direction and expressions. From movement to static-ness, from gray to color, contrasts always making the totality.

"Enough of this. These are matters to be explored individually. Drawing per se disappears into the Pattern, which creates a new look of nature.

"I think you have been doing this all the while and will continue to do it until you arrive at ONE way of visualizing it.

"But perfection or exactitude is not art, as Matisse has said. Don't think about it. Let me hear."

* * *

In September 1998 my mother broke her hip, and when I told Archie he said over the phone:

"This old age business has become a big problem; you have to give it all your attention. I remember when my father broke his hip and I helped him into bed. His eyes turned white and I thought that was the end, but it lasted another week.

"I myself can't do things like I used to, like when I get out of the bathtub I have to back out instead of my usual way. My left arm is also bothering me when I paint. I could paint with my right hand but it would be different, like when I write with it. Maybe I'll try it. Renoir used to paint with either hand."

When I told Armen the surgeon put screws in my mother's hip, she said:

"Queen Mary was also ninety-three when she broke her hip, and she was walking without a cane a year later."

Then she gave me more geriatric information.

"That's what I read about now," she said. "Old age health."

* * *

I called every few weeks in the following year, and then in the summer of 1999 Armen said Archie couldn't come to the phone.

"What do you mean 'he can't come to the phone?'"

"He can't get out of bed."

"What do you mean 'he can't get out of bed?' How does he go to the toilet?"

"He goes to the toilet but just barely."

"What did the doctor say?"

"The doctor's been on vacation."

"He's been like that for weeks and he hasn't seen a doctor?"

"He keeps saying he'll get better."

"Tell him I'd like to talk with him."

"I don't think he can make it."

It was about fifty feet from his bed to the phone in the kitchen, and I said:

"Ask him for me, please."

She told him, and then waiting for him to come to the phone she said:

"You'll have to wait; he moves very slowly."

"I'll wait."

Then there was his voice, as positive as ever, though it was very weak and soft.

"Archie," I said, "did you get the copy of my book that I mailed you?"

The Great American Loneliness had just been published, and I wanted him to see the portrait I had drawn of him that I included in it.

"Yes, we saw it. We're looking forward to big things for you."

"Archie, what's wrong? Are you sick? Armen said you're not painting anymore."

"I'm a little sick, but I'll get better."

"Stay well, Archie. I'm coming to see you in a few weeks."

"It will be good to see you. Keep painting and writing. I have to go now."

"He can't talk anymore," Armen said.

"He sounds so weak," I said.

"He is," she said.

"I'll call back in a few days. Get another doctor to come and see him."

When I called back she said he couldn't even go to the toilet.

"What do you mean, he can't even go to the toilet? What does he do?"

"He does it on himself."

"Did you get diapers?"

"I had to."

"Are you going to take him to the hospital?"

"I guess I'll have to."

"Call an ambulance."

"I guess I'll have to."

She seemed in shock, but I was shocked myself, and I was upset with her for waiting so long.

"I have to go to Fresno to care for my mother," I said. "I'll call you from there."

He was in the hospital when I called her from my mother's house.

The hospital had told her something about kidney failure and blood poisoning and that he had slipped into a coma. Holding back her tears, she said:

"Peter, they asked me if I wanted to keep him on life support."

She called the next morning while I was cooking oatmeal for my mother, and this time she was not holding back her crying anymore.

"Peter, my brother died."

"I'll get a plane as soon as I can," I said.

"You don't have to rush," she said, "I'm having him cremated."

But I wanted to rush, as if I had to be with her as soon as possible.

It was my old panic that I always imagined was like my mother's when my father had a stroke when I was only three, and though I couldn't remember that far back I always thought of it as the root of my troubled personality.

My mother in the meantime was at the end of her life and beyond all panic, and as I put down the phone I said:

"Ashod died, Ma."

She was lying in bed, weak from her heart attack, and all she said was:

"Now Ashod is gone too."

* * *

The care-taker we had hired couldn't come on weekends, and my brother, who was in San Diego, got angry when I told him he had to cut his visit short and drive back to Fresno.

"You care more about Archie," he said, "than you do your own mother!"

I booked a flight for the following midnight on Tower Airlines, the only one available.

"I have to leave tomorrow, Ma," I said. "Tommy will be here in the afternoon."

She was in those days still able to pull herself to the living room with her walker, and sitting in her chair with her mind blurred from a stroke, she said:

"Now Ashod's paintings will be worth more."

"If someone wants them," I said.

"Yes," she said, "someone has to want them."

Then she asked for the box of old photos from the closet, and her crying finally erupted as we looked at them.

"Oh Ashod!" she sobbed, "Oh Ashod!"

She sobbed deeply like a child, and I did too.

One by one we looked at the old brown photos of Ashod as a child and the later ones as a man, and then she said:

"Take them away, I don't want to cry anymore."

* * *

In San Francisco my plane was delayed until four a.m., and when I finally arrived at J.F.K the terminal of Tower Airlines was out in the boondocks.

Then blurry from no sleep, I took the wrong shuttle and was left in the middle of nowhere to wait for the right one, the gray sky and the desolate fields reminding me of all those times I was stranded in strange places in my voyage through life, and the ghost of my cousin Archie loomed over the marshes while the shock of his death made everywhere seem unreal.

I had to wait for the bus to Jamaica where I would catch the train to Patchogue, and worrying if a bus would actually come, I approached a small solitary man who stood in the vast emptiness like a figure in a dream.

There was no need to worry, he said in broken English with

a Spanish accent, he was also going to Jamaica and the bus would come soon.

He was a friendly man with the welcoming warmth of a sunny culture, and his patience comforted me.

How alive he seemed while my cousin Archie was dead, and even the bleak landscape seemed suddenly alive, though it looked like death itself.

Then I didn't have the required quarters for the bus, and slipping four from her purse a small Asian woman exchanged them for my dollar bill as if she were related to the friendly Latino.

"Thank you," I kept saying, "thank you so much." But she just nodded.

How alive she too appeared, everywhere so alive as I got closer to Bellport. There would be no funeral and only Armen would bury the ashes, but there was the friendliness of the Latino man and the Asian woman as if they were somehow part of his wake.

The bus driver said he would take me to the train station, but the Latino nudged my arm and advised me to get a transfer for a short cut.

Then waiting for the transfer in Jamaica, he said he lived near the train station and that his name was Nestor and he was from Ecuador and worked nights as a food handler in the airport and was now going home after work.

I had never been to this part of Jamaica, but the streets reminded me of my childhood in Union City, and my fatigue and grief mixed with exuberance as if Archie's ghost were guiding me.

My cousin Archie was a happy man, said the immigrant neighborhood; he had always been a happy man, and there was no need for gloom and sadness.

Then a jitney van stopped across the street, and Nestor said it would cost more but would be faster.

"I'll pay for both of us," I said.

"No," he said, he would pay.

The driver and the two other passengers were young black men, and the windows were dark like in a hearse, and loud rap music blared from the cassette player.

"It not far," Nestor said as we sat in the back, the loud rap sounding like noise to him as well.

Then a beautiful young black woman who looked like a foxy prostitute or a bold teen-ager stepped in and sat beside me, and after a few minutes of sitting next to her even the loud rap sounded good.

"Thank you so much," I said to Nestor when we were let off, "I really appreciated you guiding me here."

"I walk with you," he said. The train station was out of his way but he wanted to make sure I got to it safely.

"You don't have to," I said, "I'll be all right."

No, he insisted, Jamaica was his home now, and I was a foreign traveler to whom he must offer aid and hospitality.

Then, as if I were an illiterate peasant just off the boat, he led me to the ticket window as if he were not just Nestor now but all the other angels on my long voyage through life who had opened the doors of my heart to the other side of death.

"Thank you, Nestor!" I said, "thank you so much!

"Up there," he said, pointing to the platform for the train to Pachogue.

"Goodbye, Nestor" I said. "Thank you so much! Thank you so much!"

And he disappeared as if I had been walking with a host of friends behind the coffin of my beloved Archie and was now ready to bury it.

Archie, photo by Pete, 1994

Pete's drawing from photo, 1998

Art and Armen

And so I rode the train from Jamaica to save my cousin Archie's
paintings that he said he was leaving to me.

Looking back now, I can see of course that had I stayed in
California, it would have made no difference to their destiny, while
my panic as always would cause me even more pain.

I just got a job teaching a class in Berkeley that would start in
a few weeks, and overwhelmed with worry about my mother in
Fresno, I had to save Archie's paintings as soon as I could before I
had to return.

In the meantime, I felt I had to be with Armen as if she too
were a kind of mother who needed me, and my delusion would be
the root of my tragedy with her.

And so my story of how the paintings were taken from me really begins where I'm looking out the window of the train while she
is waiting to pick me up at the station in Patchogue and drive me
to Bellport in her old Nissan.

* * *

Who was she, the Armen I loved who was like all the other
women whose love I needed until my primal scream would drive
them all away?

We were children of a clan that had to stick together after the
massacre, but the roots of our family would wither in America like
a plant that wilts from disease, and so too would the flower of my
love for her become poisoned by my blindness.

Here now are the letters she wrote to me that year I was in
London, as I look at her delicate cursive on the blue aerograms and
sheets of onion skin as if they can reveal the secret of my pain.

She wrote well, but except for her letters to Archie during the
war, I doubt she did any other personal writing, and those to me
were only because my illiterate mother had asked her to write them
for her. They are all I have left of Armen now besides a few photos:

"May 18, Thurs. night. [1966]

Dear Peter, You will probably be surprised to hear from me, but tonight your Ma is at our home to cook her favorite 'liver' meal, and she has asked me to write a few words. Arthur has gone to Woodstock very early this year, guess he is really glad! [She had always called him 'Arthur' as if to gentrify him.]

"I read two of your letters to your mother, and they are quite charming since you describe your housekeeping habits so well, and we laughed to hear that you cook Armenian food.

[I didn't really, except for the bulghur wheat I had found in a little Turkish grocery around the corner from where I lived in Spitalfields.]

"Your Ma made such a beautiful kha-bor-gha for us at Easter. [Lamb flanks stuffed with rice.] She says you can do some cooking for her when you get home!

"As far as her pension is concerned, it is now up to the Government's decision. [The decision would be based on my mother's immigration papers, since she had no birth certificate.] We just have to wait, but she doesn't mind working at all.

"Summer has finally arrived today and she has a permanent and looks quite nice.

"Last Saturday Tom came over and showed her his new store in Oakland. [His new carpet business in Bergen County, New Jersey, after he had to leave photoengraving, which the new printing methods had supplanted.]

"The store is large and in a new shopping area. Arthur's paintings are there, but like a fool he omitted frames, which Liz [my brother's wife] thinks they should have. Guess she's right, they would probably make a better presentation. We all hope the store makes out.

"Your Ma stayed over for Mother's Day with her grandchildren who are so adorable, Peter, both of them. Melanie [age three] is so cute over the phone. She told my brother he is her best Pal. They have not forgotten you at all.

"They are very alert children. Wait till you see how they've grown. They received your books [Beatrice Potter's] and showed them to your Ma. For Mother's Day she got a Hibachi, you know, those little stoves.

"It seems that time is getting close to your homecoming. [It was my last year in London before I moved to California.] Your Ma says to throw away all old clothes, don't bring home any for her to mend, buy new ones!

"Also Tom took your Ma to the new church [near his Ridgewood home in Bergen County] where he is the one who takes around the basket for money. I have forgotten the word for it. [She never went to church herself.]

"I called Charles and Edna to wish them bon voyage to Bermuda, and I remembered you to them. Gwen [Charlie's daughter, in her teens] is alone with her grandmother [Edna's Swedish mother] and likes it since she has the rule of the house.

"Arthur and I were very elated to hear about the money you received. It must be a certain gratification to know you have some talent, and of course your Ma and my father are real proud of you. [My Stegner Fellowship at Stanford.]

"Guess I have said enough on your Ma's behalf, since she feels bad about not knowing how to write.

"Thinking of you always. Regards from all, my father especially, and Arthur.

Love Armen

[The following is from her trip with my mother to California. She was forty-five by now and had never gone anywhere before, but pushed by my mother she finally agreed. My mother liked to travel and had cousins in Pasadena as well as my brother's in-laws in San Francisco and Fresno.]

"Sept. 30, 1966
Dear Peter, We have now arrived in Pasadena and have received both your letters here.

"Our stay in San Francisco [with Tom's sister-in-law] was very nice; we visited all the notable places, even went to an art museum and planetarium. Ate in very expensive places overlooking the ocean and rode over the Golden Gate Bridge. Very picturesque. Also went to the Greenwich Village area near Berkeley.[Telegraph Avenue, which had become a tourist attraction in the Sixties.]

"Then we went to Sacramento to visit Tory. [Tory Bidinian, my mother's cousin.] We called Bill [my friend Bill Belli] but could not contact him.

"In Fresno Liz's parents were nice, but her mother is very arthritic and can't walk and is very helpless. Your mother did all the cleaning and cooking. We stayed there only three days.

"Here in Pasadena everyone is planning to take us to many places, even Mexico, so we may stay an extra week.

"I hope my brother has written you. I called home for a bit of news; it is now definite we are getting steam heat in our apartment building. [In place of the coal stoves.]

"I would love to write in detail but kinda lazy. It is easier typing. Anyhow detail is unnecessary. Just want to say that everyone adores your mother no matter where she goes.

"Love, Armen & Zarooheen [my mother's name in the family dialect.]

"[No date on a postcard from Knotts Berry Farm.]
Dear Bid, This is where we went one night. [She too sometimes used my family nickname, from Biddo, for Bedros]

"Very interesting. Had a choo-choo ride in Calico mine. Has been very warm here. But delightful. Thinking of you. Love, Armen and Zarooheen

"Oct. 7, Friday
Dear Peter, I hope you have received our letter and cards. We are now back in Pasadena and enjoying our stay. Mrs. Bidinian is very nice to us. Everyone just adores your mother, in fact everyone likes her immediately. She is so much fun. I adore her myself.

"We have been going to people's home for dinner and to a well known place in the afternoon. Your mother is going to stay another month. I am staying an extra week, four weeks in all.

"The climate here is to my liking, and I wish I could stay and live here. The way of life is so different from back east. The smog doesn't bother me but your Mom is rather annoyed by it.

"This weekend we are going to Tijuana for a day and next week we intend to go to Las Vegas. All in all your mother and I have enjoyed our stay. My being with people and getting away has made me very glad we came.

"Your mother is going to return to Fresno to stay with Liz's mother and father for a week. They have a nice place and in fact have more than I in my house. Only the mother cannot walk and it is very sad to see.

"The father is odd and at breakfast offered me liquor and a cigarette. [He was an old immigrant peasant and would live into his nineties.]

"I hope you are writing my brother. I will tell you more of our trip in person when you get back. Love, Armen and Zarooheen.

"Nov 15 Tuesday nite 6:45 [Back in New Jersey]
Dear Peter, I am at your Ma's home this evening [in North Bergen] and having dinner with her.

"She served a wonderful Porterhouse Steak with glazed carrots and French fries, and naturally we were thinking about you. Gosh we miss you, Peter, we always talk about you and think of you.

"Tom was speaking to your Ma when I got in, also Melanie and Tory. [Tom's son, age four.] They are all fine. Your Mom bought me a turkey roaster pan as a gift, and it is so large. Arthur is buying the turkey this year out of his painting money!

"It is getting rather cold and we are getting ready for the holidays. Read your last letter and enjoyed it very much. You mention a suede coat that is a real bargain since they are very expensive here, so I would purchase it if I were you. Your mother heartily approves of this. She said you should get rid of your old clothes before you get here.

"Renate [my friend] called your Ma and was inquiring about how you were since she had not heard from you, and your Ma gave her all the news. Her son started school and she is starting to teach but she said she would visit your Ma someday.

"Your Mom is getting on well. She works only two or three days a week, since the factory is slow, so she's glad to get some rest.

"I played one of your records, Vivaldi's Four Seasons, and it made her think you were here. She loves it.

"Well, time is fleeting and soon you'll be leaving England. Guess it is the best move. I envy your travels to other countries.

"We'll be thinking of you at the dinner table on Thanksgiving, Peter. Hope you have turkey too. Do they have turkey in England?

"Lots of love from everyone and of course especially from me. Armen and Zarooheen

"June 18, Sunday [Spring 1967]
Dear Peter, your mother has induced me to write you since I am closest to her, but it is a pleasure.

"She is working as usual and still hasn't heard from the Social Security Board but thinks they will accept the 'Boat Proof' soon.

"It has been very hot in N.Y. and quite unbearable. This is the only season of the year that I hate.

"I'm surprised you do not have too much to carry, but that is good. Hope you have someone to pick you up. If it's on a Sunday Tom can pick you up.

"I know you will miss England where the life and people are so different. But you can always go back, you have no possessions or responsibilities, and even if you did, that should not stand in the way.

"So until I see you again, Love, Armen

"P.S. It will be nice to see you again even though I am not on your intellectual level!"

* * *

I have only a few photos of her, since she hated being photographed. In one of the old black and white photos, she is standing with my mother and Archie at what must have been the graduation party for Archie when he was twelve and she was six, and I imagine her dress is the one my mother had sewn for her that she would remember for the rest of her life. The helmet Archie is wearing

Zaroohe, Armen, Archie

must have been from the First
World War, though I have no
idea where he got it.

In another she is stand-
ing beside my father with my
brother on his shoulders at
Coney Island when she was
about fourteen, and though
she was chubby then she
would be trim with a perfect
figure for the rest of her life.
[see page 64.]

In a later color photo she
is sitting beside my mother
and Edna with Archie and Charlie behind them in the kitchen in
Bellport. It is from the fall of 1978 when she had just turned fif-
ty-eight and my mother was visiting back east.

Edna, Charlie, Zaroohe, Archie, Armen, Bellport, 1978

She had big bright eyes and sensual lips and a small straight nose she had inherited from her father, and though she was attractive she had the hair above her lip removed by electrolysis when she was quite young.

Since image was everything to her, she had always been hypersensitive to anyone looking at her, especially when she was only fifteen and older men would leer at her.

"They were always looking at me," she would tell me one night, alluding to someone who wanted more than a look as if he were disgusting.

She didn't start "going out" until after the war. She was twenty when it started and most of the young men had been drafted, nor was it easy for young women to be sexual in those days when most stayed with their parents until they married, especially in immigrant families.

But she did enjoy working in Manhattan where she would often see someone famous on Madison Avenue, like Greta Garbo.

She loved dressing up and was always out on Saturday nights, either at an Armenian affair or a bar with friends, where she too would smoke cigarettes and nurse a scotch and soda, though she hated smoking until she was finally able to quit in her forties.

She did date of course, and when I was a teen I saw one of her suitors when he visited her in Union City, but I don't know anyone she may have slept with. She may have spent an occasional weekend away from home, but the rest is a mystery.

My brother remembers she once went out with one of his former schoolmates who was ten years younger than she, but that's all he knows.

She was sexy and could be friendly, and her dauntless side could emerge if she were pushed, as it was when she had to learn how to drive, but her timid side was dominant, and my mother practically had to drag her to California where she would never have gone alone.

We had different personalities but were very similar in our insecurity and sensitivity, and I could more than sympathize with the trauma of her childhood and her mother's cancer, while I too had my fearful side in a world where I felt so alone.

She was a soft and gentle woman whom everyone liked, yet she had an anger that no one saw but me, and it emerged in her old age when she became hard and bitter about becoming so isolated.

And so hearing her worry about money after Archie's S.S.I. was gone, I would tell her to get a reverse mortgage and spend it in the rest of her years. I certainly didn't want to inherit her property, I said. The thought of inheritance more than disturbed me, since I had been worrying about money all my life and was horrified by the thought of greed.

"Please, Armen," I would say, "get a reverse mortgage and stop worrying. Buy yourself a new car and all the other things you always wanted."

But she never would.

Why not? What was she thinking? Who was the Armen I loved and yet really didn't know? Why didn't she get that reverse mortgage and leave nothing of the property that would cause not only my tragedy with her but with Little Aram as well?

I still have the blue metal box she gave me that Christmas when I was a child and she visited my mother's home for the first time after my brother's grandmother had died and the ban from my mother's divorce was lifted.

How happy her gift made me! It was a carpenter's box for children with a small but real hammer and saw and screw driver and chisel.

"Handy Andy Tool Set," it says as I look at the little illustration of a man with a hammer and saw, "mfg'd by Skil-Craft Corp. Chicago." Najar is an ancient Akkadian word that means carpenter, and the box has always felt like a talisman to me.

I fill it now with my old family photos as if it will protect them when the earthquake hits, the gift from my beloved cousin Armen, as if she really did love me.

And when I was eight years old it was she who took me to the Circus in the old Madison Square Garden and Roy Rogers was there with his horse Trigger! And Archie bought me a ring made of lead that cost twenty-five cents that was from the finger of the biggest man on earth who was nine feet tall and let me shake his enormous hand!

How excited I was to be treated to something so fabulous!

And when I got lost in the crowd and panicked as only a child can panic at losing his parents, there she was finding me, and how relieved and safe I felt with her!

How could she not love me when I loved her so deeply?

Zaroohe and Armen, Bellport, 1978

* * *

Then there she was standing on the platform at Patchogue when I stepped off the train, and we walked to her old Nissan.

It was in August and her birthday had just passed and mine was about to come, but she wouldn't mention it. She had just turned seventy-nine and had finally let her hair stay gray instead of dying it, her figure still trim and limber, though she still walked as if on eggs.

She looked very glum and not at all happy to see me, why I didn't know. Maybe because she was still in shock from Archie's death, but I wasn't sure.

What was she thinking, what was she feeling, the same question I always asked about all the women I loved who didn't love me back?

We chatted superficially over a simple dinner, and then exhausted from my flight I fell asleep in Archie's bed, my head by the same wall as hers on the other side of it, just as his had been.

Then in the morning I plunged into my task with my old panic as if the world would end if I didn't finish in time, and it was my panic that would lead to how the very paintings I was trying to save would be virtually stolen from me, as if there was nothing I could do to hold back the wheels of their destiny.

"I didn't know how I was going to deal with them," she said as she watched me plunge into the mess with the black plastic trash bags for what would go to the dump or the Salvation Army.

"You're just like your mother," she said as I worked non-stop, which I took as a compliment until she would later say I was nothing like my father who was a gentle man who never raised his voice.

We had never lived alone together, and my anger would be the same as when I raised my voice with the women I never married.

I loved her, yes, and yes, she did once have a kind of love of me, and why she would eventually betray me may have really been my own fault.

"Are you going to throw that out?" she said as if to scold me when I came across something she wanted to keep.

"No!" I shouted, "I won't throw anything out before asking you! Go away and leave me be!"

"Oh, those magazines," she said when I came to the Playboys and Penthouses. "Throw them out!"

He had used them in place of models for the same reason artists had always used models, and I thought of what Renoir said about painting with his "prick" and what Charlie had said when I last saw him at Christmas time:

"It still gets hard," he giggled.

There were also her Victoria Secret catalogues and his horse magazines and books and piles of who knew what, as if I were in the Augean Stables that would take a Hercules to clean, the mess like the rubble after the quake in Armenia when I dug to find a sign of life and found the leg of a dead girl buried in the dust.

Here now in the little bedroom the coldness of the dead girl's flesh became the death of my cousin Archie in his old cans and brushes and underwear and socks, and I stuffed them into the plastic bags and piled them on the front lawn.

Then after ripping away the old carpet and laying it on the pile of bags, I washed the floor and stacked the works on paper and Masonite in the corners and on his mother's old foot-peddle sewing machine he had used for a table, filling in the meantime the empty closet with those on stretched canvas.

Seeing me work in the frenzy of my panic, she said, "Oh, just put it all in the garbage."

"Are you crazy!" I shouted.

"Well, that's what he told me," she said. "He said just leave it for the garbage."

She was probably nagging him and he meant of course if I couldn't come back to deal with it.

"Just leave me alone," I said, "and stop nagging me!"

"I'm not nagging you," she said, "don't you ever call me a nag!"

But finally done, I showered and rested and we had a quiet dinner, and I went to sleep in what was now a storage room with a bare wooden floor like a way station where Archie's paintings were stacked around me like his ghost.

At least he didn't suffer, they said. He loved his work and his life let him continue until he fell into a coma instead of lingering in a nursing home.

The garage would take the next few days, and though most of it was still dry, more than half of the early work had become too moldy to save, and I had to pile it with the rug and the garbage bags.

There was more squabbling with Armen as she watched how exhausted I grew and kept telling me to leave it all, but the evenings passed quietly until I finally cleared the garage and stacked everything under plastic sheets.

Then came my panic about how to haul what I had piled on the front lawn. The neighbor across the road had mistakenly told us the town would haul it away, and after another neighbor complained a young policeman arrived to say we would be fined if it weren't cleared in the next few days.

No, he said, he didn't know of anyone we could pay, and there was no one in the local yellow pages.

Panicked, I said to Armen, "You lived here for twenty-five years and you don't know anyone we can ask about how to find someone?"

And this led to another of our squabbles.

I almost broke down when the policeman returned, and when he saw how helpless I felt he called his headquarters.

"We have an old woman here," he said over the phone, "and her cousin is old himself."

I felt insulted, but I heaved a sigh of relief when he said the town would make an exception and send its garbage truck.

It arrived in a short while, and when the two workers began dumping the pile into the truck I asked them to leave the moldy paintings to me.

Then there it was, the black hole of the garbage truck like the black hole of the universe where all would disappear including the universe itself, and into it I dumped the years in Woodstock and in Union City when he would write to me of his progress, the truck driving away as if it were the hearse that wouldn't be needed for his body.

Now I had to find a photographer for the slides I would need for galleries, and after searching in another panic I found one in Patchogue who would come to the bungalow but said it would cost five hundred dollars, which was more than Armen and I could afford.

The following day Charlie came with Little Aram and Lillian, but they could stay only for lunch to avoid traffic on the way back.

I was more than happy to see them, and Armen was too. I loved my cousin Aram as if he were my older brother, and though I didn't know Lillian well I had a kind of love for her too.

"What are you worrying about five hundred dollars for?" Aram said, "I pay that much to take my clients to lunch. Just tell the photographer to send me the bill. I'll put it on my expense account."

He had plenty of property and was about to retire when he suddenly landed some big accounts as a salesman for a printer, so he had decided to keep working.

"I didn't realize Archie had so much work," Charlie said when I showed him the room and the garage.

Then we all squeezed around the table in the tiny kitchen for the hokee josh, hokee for soul and josh for meal, the meal for the soul, and I felt as if Archie's ghost had spread his wings around us like the holy dove.

We were a family, I thought, the family I always wanted, and my illusion would turn into my tragedy.

Zaroohe holding Archie's painting, Bellport, 1978

Art and The Galleries

That evening, after Charlie, Aram and Lillian left, I asked Armen to help me choose the paintings for the slides, and she sat on the remaining cushion of the couch as I showed her the pile of what I thought was the best of Archie's work, the other cushion soiled and discarded from when he hadn't been able to rise for the toilet.

My panic was over and my mission accomplished, the best of his work stuffed in his room and the rest safe in the garage. I would leave in the morning and the photographer would take what we chose to her studio and mail me the slides in Berkeley for when I would return in the spring to show them to galleries.

Now Armen and I could relax and enjoy each other, I thought, and she did seen to enjoy choosing the paintings with me. We loved Archie and we loved his work, and looking at it together seemed to bring us closer than we had ever been before, or so I thought, and I went to bed that night looking forward to my return when we could finally be happy together.

With my mother almost gone, Armen was all I had left, and as I fell asleep I thought of how happy I would be sleeping with my head on the other side of the wall from hers like I had done with my mother, and Archie's room would be like my own.

She too seemed relaxed that night, but in the morning when we stopped at the Salvation Army to unload the old clothes and leftovers, she looked glum again, and I couldn't tell why.

She looked so old and frail I wanted to hold her and protect her and tell her not to worry and that I would always be with her just as I was with my mother, but she looked back as if in shrinking into her old shell she was closing the valves of her heart like stone.

What was she thinking? What was she feeling?

Then at the station I wanted to hug her with love but wanted even more for her to hug me back, yet no one in our family ever really hugged except my mother, and instead it would always be like when you touch a small bird, and so too did I bend shyly to kiss her cheek, and she shrank like a bird as if...as if what?

Why was she looking so hard and frozen?

The following are from some of the slides of the selected paintings, oil on canvas [color altered by reproduction]

It was the last look I would have of her for the rest of our lives, and I think now that it was at that moment she began shrinking into the shell of her bitterness, and it would not be until she became demented that she would remember her love for me and forget that I had even been to Bellport at all.

"I'll call you," I said as I turned to board the train, but she just nodded and walked back to her car.

* * *

The following autumn was very heavy for both my brother and me when his wife Elise was suffering from cancer and our mother was bedridden, and I had to drive to Fresno every weekend until we could finally put my mother into a nursing home.

Then at the beginning of the following year, 2000, I called Armen to say I was coming east with the slides and would stay with her again.

"I don't want you to come here," she said.

Shocked, I said, "What do you mean you don't want me to come there?"

"I don't want you to come here," she said, "you can stay somewhere else."

"I don't have anywhere else," I said, "my friend Bobby moved in with his girlfriend and I can't stay with him in Manhattan anymore."

"You can find someone else," she said.

"What are you talking about," I said, "have you gone nuts?"

And then there it was again, my old anger that would push her further into her shell.

Yet she had said the same to Sonya, who had been her closest friend and wanted to come and say good-bye before emigrating to Greece.

Why did she even not want to see Sonya, as if she were already becoming deranged? Who was she now whom Sonya and I would never see again, as if the destiny of Archie's paintings were tied to her derangement that would grow worse each year?

And so I called Aram, but he said I couldn't stay with him

either because his spare rooms were full, which I thought very odd, not knowing it was because Lillian had become a hoarder who had stuffed all their spare rooms with her plastic bags, which I will describe in a later chapter.

"You can stay in my office," Aram said, just as he had said he would pay the photographer, "I'll give you the key."

His so-called office was a furnished studio apartment in a building he owned in Richfield in Bergen County that he called his office as a write-off, but it felt dismal to me, and I stayed instead in Montclair with my friend Carmela who lived near the bus to Manhattan.

* * *

Montclair was on the other side of what is now called the meadowlands, but when I was kid in Union City we called them "the dumps" where the garbage trucks dumped all the garbage of our neighborhoods that were left in the cans on the sidewalk.

Growing up in Union City I had never come out this far, yet I always felt the presence of the marshland and the river that ran through it, like when we were kids and would suck the stalks of the cattails as if they were cigars and their brown fur would feel wild and exotic.

The marshland lay below the cliffs where I often played, and from there I could see the small mountains in the west as if they were another America where the great sky and wide open spaces were what I would later love most in painting plein air.

Like my cousin Archie I was a city boy, but I too would love what was called the "country," from *terra contrata*, the land lying opposite. The city was great, but I had always longed for somewhere else.

It was what Armen had meant when she first moved to Bellport and said to me with a happy gleam in her eye:

"It's like living in the country."

And so the bus now turned east from Montclair toward Manhattan, and as it passed over the marshes and the Hackensack River I could see through the window the same cat-tails of my youth as if I were riding through my life, when suddenly the bus turned from the highway up the hill into Union City, where it would take more passengers before turning into the Lincoln Tunnel.

Oh Bus, said my heart, thank you, thank you!

I had always stayed in Manhattan after my friend Bobby moved there, and decades had passed since I had seen the streets of my childhood.

They had become Hispanic by now, but Bergenline Avenue was the same, and so too the road to the tunnel down the cliff in Weehawken, where as Joyce would say in his great short story, *Araby*: "we played till our bodies glowed."

The old barges and rail cars were gone, but the river too was the same, and Manhattan was still shining on the other shore like an enchanted fairyland, the great boulders and layers of slate rising like totemic monuments.

Then came the familiar tunnel that had replaced the ferry of Archie's youth, and in just a few minutes I was in Port Authority Terminal, carrying the slides of his paintings that Armen and I had chosen.

And as I walked up Eighth Avenue the sun was rising above the rooftops and the red brick of the buildings were aglow in the shafts of light with their windows beveled by shadows like in a painting by Edward Hopper, and the shopkeepers were hosing the sidewalks like a morning ablution.

And when I came to the corner of Forty-Sixth Street that was now called Jewelry Street, I looked up to an office where I imagined my father once twisted silver into his own kind of snakes, or so my brother and my cousin Aram once told me when they remembered him giving them a coin for ice-cream cones.

My father's office must have been by Sixth Avenue and not Eighth, and yet as I looked up at the corner building I imagined it was the same as when he was the whole man for whom I would pray when I lit my candle every Sunday morning before visiting my cousin Archie who would take his place as my father figure, and I was carrying the slides of Archie's paintings as if to sell them like his own kind of jewelry.

And so too was I walking the same route as that morning in my childhood when I had played hooky to join him on his gallery tour and we saw de Kooning in the Janis Galllery, and once again I stopped at the Art Students League across from the newly cleaned Carnegie Hall on Fifty-Seventh Street, just as we had done so long ago.

Art, art, art, always art, his very name was Art, and so did he sign his paintings: "Art Pinajian, artist."

"You let Ashod fill Biddo's head with all that art garbage," Aram's mother Manooshag once said to my mother in Armenian, scolding my mother for letting me become like Ashod, and Manooshag used the Turkish word for garbage that had a particular nasty ring to it: "zibil."

The League was smaller than I remembered from when Archie had brought me here, and as I peeked into one of the studios on the way to its gallery the studio was smaller and different from what I remembered, as if I hadn't been here at all, yet how could that be when my memory was so vivid?

The League's gallery, said the manager, was only for students and instructors, but she was sympathetic to my slides and wished me well, and so I left and continued up the street.

The galleries of Fifty-Seventh Street had been in my youth like the entrance to fame and fortune where only the chosen were admitted, but as I passed them now they looked as dreary and vain as an old movie star who had grown wrinkled and grey.

My friend Lenny Silverberg had written a list of the uptown galleries who might be interested in Archie's kind of work, and the first on my route was the Tatischeff, where the director seemed as sympathetic as the one in the League after I showed him the war sketches and the comics.

"Estates are very difficult to handle," he said. "You should try the galleries in the Hamptons, since your cousin's work looks local."

On the walls hung some academic landscapes in the kind of realism that Archie had eschewed, and I realized what I was up against, just as he had been.

A few doors down at the Fishbach Gallery the director was the opposite of sympathetic and didn't even want to glance at the slides or the sketches.

"We don't represent estates," he scoffed, as if I were a salesman who had passed a no soliciting sign.

He had an ashen face that suddenly looked like Boris Karloff's in the first Frankenstein film, and I wanted to snarl: *You piece of shit;* but I walked away in silence.

The current show at the Fishbach was of sentimental land-scapes that suddenly became disgusting because of how insulted I felt, but my anger, I realized, was not for Archie's sake but my own.

I was not showing the slides for him but for myself. Archie was gone and couldn't care anymore if his work was shown or not; I was the one who cared, as if my own life were at stake.

And so it went up Fifty-Seventh Street and then Madison Avenue, following the list Lenny had written for me, and each gallery would say no in their different ways.

"We're not looking for any new artist's work," said the snobby receptionist at the Michael Rosenfeld Gallery.

"We already have our stable of artists," said the young man at the Zabriskie Gallery, as if artists were racing horses and the gallery owners, managers and clerks were all betting on them.

"This doesn't interest me," said the imperious woman with the thick Eastern European accent in the Katharina Rich Perlow Gallery, who must have been Katharina herself.

Had I been less serious she would have seemed as comic as a Dickens caricature, but once again I felt insulted as she looked up at my face and talked down to my pride.

"You can't show them like this!" she said, as if I were a school-boy. "They have to have dates on them! Where are the dates?"

Then glancing at the war sketches and the comics, she said:

"Where are the paintings from this period? I might be interested in them for historical reasons""

And behind her were some paintings in a minimalist style that were in fashion then.

The receptions were more polite however at the Moore and the Tibor de Nagy galleries, though each director also said sorry, they were not taking anything new.

Then at the Babcock Gallery the assistant director was a friendly man who was the only one to look at the slides carefully, but he
too finally said no.

"The other night," he said, "there was a documentary on television about war artists."

At the Maxwell Gallery the old director was about to turn me
away when his eye spotted the Battle of the Bulge on my short
biography.

"I was in the Bulge myself," he said proudly, and he showed
me the photo on his desk of him and his buddy in the winter of
'44, each of them in khaki.

"I'll tell you what," he said, as if doing a favor for an old
buddy, "I'll refer you to someone else. Your cousin's paintings are
modern art and we carry only conventional work. What was his
name again?"

And he looked it up in a big black book and then a big red one
that were registries of credentials.

"No," he said, "I can't help you, your cousin's name is not even
in the book."

Then he turned to greet a fancy couple that had just come
through the door as if they had big bucks to spend.

* * *

Yes, these galleries were what my Archie had been up against,
and though I had always known of them, I now faced them first-
hand, and by the time I reached Eightieth Street I surrendered.

The only book of his true credentials would be my own, and it
too would face what Blake had called "the desolate market where
none come to buy."

It was mid-afternoon by now, and since I had come as far as
Eightieth Street I walked to the Met and ate my cheese sandwich
on the steps outside.

Luckily the sun was shining and I was grateful to be alive, but
the business of art had tired and depressed me, and I needed to rest
and revive before moving on.

"I come here like going to church," Charlie had said about the

Met, and I always felt the same, as if I were a boy who once lit a candle under a Madonna for my father to be whole again.

The Met was not as large as the Louvre or as intimate as the National Gallery in London, yet it was my favorite of all museums, and I walked to my secret couch in the Lehman wing.

It was in a little room where few would wander, and by luck no one was sitting there. It was small like the couch Armen bought with my friend Bobby's money, though much older, and I wouldn't have been able to sprawl on it with someone else on the next cushion.

In the old days there were couches everywhere in the Met, but this was the only one left, and I felt it was especially for me.

There was an old oriental carpet on the floor and an antique cabinet as if in a private study, and the couch too was old and soft as if it had also survived the centuries like an idyllic pastoral.

It was the year 2000, the beginning of a new century, and turning sixty I lived in a small cottage in Berkeley where I hadn't enjoyed a couch since I was a kid, and I sank into the soft cushions as if were in my childhood on that old musty couch by the potbelly stove in the little parlor that Archie had used for a studio.

It was Friday and the Met would stay open until nine, so there was no worry about a guard kicking me out before I had my fill, and I sprawled on the couch looking up at the great Rembrandt of a Dutch merchant and the two El Grecos of a Jesus with a cross and St. Jerome with his Bible, the bag of the slides at my side as if they. were Archie himself with his bent fingernail pointing at the panels of Prince Valiant.

We had never come to the Met together, in fact we were rarely together after I had grown, and I never even saw him in the act of painting except for the little life study of me when I was fifteen and he had imitated Picasso by using only earth tones.

It didn't look like me, and yet it was "modern art," and it caught my youth and awkwardness.

He was a modern artist who survived as best he could so he could continue painting, and in another age he might have worked in a master's studio or may have even been a master himself, and further back he might have been employed by a church or a temple;

and even further back he may have even followed a shaman into a cave or may have been a shaman himself.

Now he was gone and I was in a cave of all the ages, and the pictures on its walls were the story I had been trying to write since I first fell in love with them.

"It is between me and myself that I work now," he had said.

"My work is a reflection of what I want my life to be.

"To understand the totality of art is to arrive at its creation.

"If you are conscious of Totality, time will coalesce everything into one.

"Searching for forms is terrific therapy and makes me feel good and refreshed. No one notices, of course, except the creator and sometimes not even he."

It was young Doris Barbalinardo who first brought me to the Met when I was a child. She was eight years older than I and I thought of her as my big sister, and she still calls me from her home by the Jersey Shore.

She lived on the ground floor of our apartment building on Bergenline Avenue, and one day when she was in high school and I was about eight, she brought me here because she too was in love with art, and it was this love we would always have in common.

And so I felt at home here as if I were with Doris and Archie and everyone else who shared the same love, as if they were all my sangha on my path to awakening from the dream we called life.

Then rested and revived, I continued to what were also called galleries, as if they were the history of humanity, and I came to one of Mesopotamia that was supposed to be the cradle of our civilization.

And it had the little figure from *Tell Asmar* that I attach with this chapter, whose hypnotic stare de Kooning was supposed to have copied in his paintings on paper I had seen with Archie in what felt like a chapel in my epiphany.

The little figure seemed to be praying, and so too did I once pray when I was a child until I stopped when my father died, yet from then on my life in art was also a kind of prayer, as if my love for it were a kind of hero worship.

Then suddenly a guard was standing nearby as I looked from the little Mesopotamian figure to his face.

He was a middle-aged Italian immigrant whose smile brought me back to the here and now through which Joyce had said, "all future plunges into the past," and I remembered what Blake had said about worship and prayer:

"God appears and God is light, to those poor souls who dwell in night, but does a human form display to those who live in realms of day."

"How's the wedda outside?" said the guard who had been inside all day.

"Great," I said, "you should step out on your break."

"I'm gettin off at five-dirty," he said, "and den I'm gettin out a dis place."

From Tel Asmar

Art and Inheritance

A *ram's wife Lillian* must have learned of my trouble with Armen when I told him Armen didn't want me to stay in Bellport on my visit.

She and Armen weren't close, and from what I know about Lillian now, she must have called Armen as if to show concern about her being alone after Archie was gone, though neither had ever called each other before.

As if by destiny, her son John, who was forty-two by now, had been commuting to the Island as part of his business as a salesman, so Lillian told him to visit Armen and see if he could be of any help to her.

Armen hadn't seen him since he was a child, but he had turned out to be a friendly man, and she let him take her shopping and even help her buy a newer car.

Then in the following July of 2001, Armen would sign a will leaving her estate to him and his sister and parents with him as the executor, which I wouldn't know about until six years later when a copy of the will was sent by the Suffolk County courthouse to Charlie and me in case we wanted to contest it, since we were Armen's first cousins and Aram was only her second cousin.

Yet Charlie and I would have said nothing about the will when Armen signed it, so there was really no need for Aram to lie about it to my brother when Tom happened to visit back east.

Armen was more fond of my brother than Aram, and Tom was much closer to her, but Tom was only her distant cousin by blood and could have done nothing about the will, nor would Charlie's daughter Gwen have said anything about it, though Armen was more fond of her than John, whom she hardly knew.

So Aram's deception was really unnecessary, unless it may have also been because he felt some guilt, which I would never know.

And who knows what Armen was thinking when she signed that will? She was very afraid of being alone in her old age, especially since Tom and Gwen and I were all so far away in California, so Lillian and John may have convinced her that they would look after her.

Yet John would stop commuting to the Island soon after the will was signed and never see Armen again, and Lillian would stop calling her.

I of course would continue calling her for the rest of her life, and though she was aloof at first, she would forget in her dementia that I had even been with her when Archie died, and her bad feelings about me would disappear like her home itself.

"Peter," she would say to me over the phone in her final weeks, "They want to take away my home."

"Who's 'they'?" I said.

"You know who," she said like a child.

"No, I don't. Who are you talking about?"

But all she wanted to talk about was her childhood and the dress my mother sewed for her and that my brother was really my father's son.

But I am getting ahead of my story and must return to that spring of 2000 after I took the slides to the galleries and met Aram for lunch on the following day.

I always saw him when I went back east, since he was like an older brother to me. His mother Manooshag was like my second mother, and I would honor her in my book about my mother. My mother and she were like sisters and I called her my aunt, though her father was my father's older brother.

My father and Archie's mother and Charlie's mother were the only ones left of the Najarian family after the massacre, and each of their names were in our grandfather's Bible that she said she was leaving to me because I was the last Najarian.

I will write in my last chapter of how she came to have this Bible and how important the Najarian name was to her.

It was a clean name, my mother would tell me, using the Armenian word for clean: "*mah-kur*."

A mah-kur name was more important than anything else, my mother would say, and the Najarian family never had anything to be ashamed of.

And I really do believe that had Manooshag been alive after Armen made her will, she would have stopped Aram from virtually stealing not only Archie's paintings from me but the very Bible with our names in it.

Aram was not completely a bad person, my brother would say: "He was pussy whipped by Lillian."

Manooshag, Zaroohe & Tom

But even good people do bad things, especially when it comes to inheritance.

Tom and Aram had grown up like brothers, and Manooshag liked my brother so much that she, like Armen, wanted to believe he was my father's son, though in honor of my mother Manooshag never mentioned this.

And so, since our Najarian family was so close, it was only natural that I would ask Aram to keep an eye on Archie's paintings after Armen didn't want me come to Bellport anymore.

He had a meeting with a client in Manhattan, and we met by the steps to the Met where he parked his new BMW in the Met's garage, and he asked me where a good place might be to have lunch.

I never ate out, I said, especially around the Met where the restaurants were all expensive, but he said he didn't care about money anymore, so we found one around the corner on Madison Avenue.

I worried about Archie's paintings, I said, and he said his son John would keep an eye on them.

Then as I walked him to his BMW in the parking garage, he continued talking about his son John and his daughter Lori. They were everything to him and he would do anything for them.

John had bought another house in Ridgewood and Lori was doing well in Oradell, though she had her hands full with her two sets of twins, whom Aram adored.

John was born in 1958 when I left for college, and Lori was born just before I left for London, so I had seen them rarely as the years went by, but I would always make a special effort to visit them on my trips back east as if they were my niece and nephew.

Then arriving at his new BMW, which was the biggest model, Aram said it was just one of his "toys."

He liked to play the big shot, and his affable personality was part of why he was so good a salesman, the other part was his drive and his energy.

He was a voracious reader, and one of his favorite books in his youth was Budd Shulberg's *What Makes Sammy Run*; but I didn't read it until after the betrayal, and when I discovered it too was a betrayal story I wondered if Aram really admired Sammy despite his ruthlessness?

Yes, the hurt I feel now is because I loved Aram so deeply, and my tragedy stems from my blindness of not truly knowing him, just as I didn't really know Armen who had betrayed me even more deeply.

Aram was even my godfather because he had been the best man when my father married my mother in his home when he was only five, and when I was born three years later, his father had to hold his arms above the basin at my baptism.

This baptism story would be repeated in our family as if it were part of our family Bible, and so I grew up loving Aram as my "god-father," which was in the olden days such an honored title. Yes, I loved him, just as I loved Armen, my cousin Aram, who was called "Little Aram" because he was born after Charlie's older brother, "Big Aram."

And he was, yes, very lovable, with bright eyes and a winning personality, and I would ignore the other side of him that needed to act like a big shot as if to make up for how small he really felt.

His mother had miscarried so many times she had to lie on her back for months so he could be born; then he was such a small and delicate baby he was pampered and coddled.

His father Vahan had been a hero in the French Volunteer force of Armenians who fought the Turks in Jerusalem, and Aram wanted to be like his father, an honorable and generous man who dictated to me his memoir that I would use in my first novel.

He was short like his father and much too short for basketball, yet he was a natural athlete and played varsity and was also a star shortstop. Then he was so good in golf he would play in tournaments.

He married Lillian after he came home from Korea, where he had seen only limited combat before the war ended in '53. She was a few years younger, and I actually knew her before he did.

She was a very pretty girl with big beautiful green eyes, and I knew her in my childhood by her Armenian name, Shushanig, from *shusan* for lily, pronounced "shoo-shan-eeg."

Her mother was a sweet woman who had nightmares of blood from the horrors she had witnessed in the massacre, and her father had been a jeweler who shared my father's shop on Jewelry Street, and she was related on her father's side to Peter Balakian, who would write about his grandmother Nafinah in the genocide, and Nafinah, I was told, was a distant relative of the Najarians.

Aram and Lillian's daughter Lori was born the same year as my brother's son and a year before my brother's daughter, and the three children would play together when they visited my mother, whom they each adored.

Yes, we were a family, or so I thought, and after Aram's mother and father died, he would lay flowers not only on their graves every Memorial Day, but on my father's grave as well, and I wonder now if he still does.

And when he came out west for a golf tournament at Pebble Beach, he made a special trip to Fresno to see my brother and mother before seeing me in San Francisco.

He was a good boy, my mother would always say of him, and she would die never knowing about Armen's will or what happened to Archie's paintings.

And so returning to Berkeley in that spring of 2000, I called Aram about them.

They're okay, Aram said, "Johnny's looking out for them."

And when I emailed John to send me some canvases that I might offer to galleries, he had packaged a few for me and shipped from the printing company where Aram was a salesman.

Then out of the blue one day John emailed a strange reply in which he said he and his mother didn't want to be involved in anything between me and Armen anymore, and when I told this to my brother, Tom asked me:

"What's Lillian got to do with Armen?"

Tom knew Lillian better than I and had already seen her spare rooms stuffed with big plastic trash bags full of old clothes she couldn't let go of.

Yes, something had happened between Lillian and Armen, but I had to push it out of my mind, since what could I do about it anyway?

When I called Armen she didn't want to talk about the paintings, and when I told her how hurt I felt by her coldness, she said:

"Yes, I know how you feel, I know what it's like to be rejected."

But who had rejected her? Was he one of her boyfriends? And had I become his scapegoat?

And when she didn't want to talk about the paintings over the phone, I wrote to her that I had sent the slides and copies of the comics and war drawings to museums in Long Island and Montclair and Newark and that I showed them to galleries in San Francisco and needed to return to Bellport to bring some back, since those that Johnny sent was not the best of his work.

And she replied in a note, dated October 29, 2001, four months after she signed the will that I didn't know about:

"Dear Peter, Received your letter and the picture of your mother. It is very sad to see her at that age.

"Actually I am not interested in the past. I am just interested in my current surrounding and existence.

"The people I loved have gone and I now have no one!

"Anything that I have in regard to my brother will be with Aram in New Jersey. Go pick up anything you want from there.

"There is no necessity of coming to Bellport.

"Forget the past! Your cousin, Armen"

Aram did tell me he had taken about half a dozen of Archie's early work to hang in his summer home in Belmar, and he didn't know why Armen wrote as if he had the rest of the paintngs, which were all still in the garage and in Archie's room where I had stacked them.

Johnny was no longer commuting to Long Island, Aram said, but he was sure the paintings were still safe.

In the meantime there was nothing I could do short of flying east and confronting Armen, which would have been a disaster. And so I continued trying to promote Archie's work while editing his letters for the biography I was writing about him.

In the meantime my brother flew east for the wedding of a friend's daughter, and he met Aram for lunch, which Tom told me about when he returned to Fresno.

"I asked Aram what was happening with Armen's house," Tom said, "but he was very evasive and said only that she made a living trust and Johnny has power of attorney, "

Aram of course lied about the will, but not knowing this, I had to ignore whatever the living trust meant, since what could I have done about it anyway? If Armen's house was in Aram's hands, so be it, all I cared about were the paintings, and I trusted Aram would let me have them, especially since he thought they were worthless.

As the years passed I continued to call Armen until one day there was a strange voice on an answering machine that she never had before. And after I left an urgent message, a young woman called me back and said she was a neighbor whose family had been caring for Armen who was bedridden.

The neighbors had been using Armen's checkbook for a care-giver to live in Archie's room, and when I called Aram to ask about this, Lillian answered the phone.

Then Lillian was not only as shocked as I, but very angry, and it was then I learned she had been out of touch with Armen for several years.

And so Lillian and Aram rushed to Bellport, and when I called them, Lillian told me she got a court order to kick the neighbors out, and she hired a private nurse to stay in Archie's room.

What happened to the paintings that were in the room, I asked, and she said the neighbors had put them in the garage.

It was during this period that Armen had sunk so deep in her dementia that she had forgotten I had ever been there, and she died soon after with the cancer in her lungs spreading to her brain until she was no longer coherent.

Aram had her cremated, he said, but I neglected to ask what he did with the ashes. She had buried Archie's ashes in a grave near Bellport, but I wouldn't learn if hers were there as well.

Worried about the paintings, I had to fly back east as soon as I could.

My mother died in March of 2006, and Lillian sent a condolence card and then a note along with a form from the Suffolk County Court, her penmanship with the same cursive as Armen's that we all learned in school in those days.

"Dear Peter, Sorry for any inconvenience, but New York Courts are very strict when it comes to probating wills. They want to make sure that Armen has no living children or other brothers or sisters. We are enclosing your expenses for the Notary Public and for postage.

"We are making a donation to Holy Cross Church in memory of your mother. We have many fond memories of her. As children she always gave us a lot of attention and was very fun to be with. She was far ahead of her time in her thinking and she certainly was a survivor during her difficult times. We, along with John and Lori, enjoyed watching the video of the documentary about her. She had a full life and was able to make anyone who knew her enjoy her company. She will be greatly missed. Love, Aram and Lillian."

Looking back now, I can't believe I was so stupid as to think there had been no will and that one had been drawn in which Charlie and I and my brother and Gwen would be included, since we were all family and that's what I would have done, or how else could I explain to myself why Lillian trusted me so openly?

And so I stupidly signed the form saying yes, Aram was Armen's cousin, and I didn't use Lillian's check but paid the notary myself as well as the postage for registered mail. Charlie however never received the form or was beyond comprehending it, since he was over ninety by then and his memory was jumbled.

I realize now of course that Lillian and Aram must have found it equally incredible that I could be so stupid not to have assumed Armen had already made her will. I must have seemed so indifferent to anything but the paintings that they trusted I would sign the form so they could enter the property where the paintings were still in the garage.

They actually must have wanted to believe, I realize now, that Armen left her home to them because she had bad feelings for me and because Lori had four kids and the rest of our family wouldn't need it.

Yet when I called Aram to say I was flying east, I thought it very strange that he asked me why I was going to so much trouble when the paintings were worthless, and he sounded as if he didn't want me to come.

Looking back now, I think he may have suspected I had something up my sleeve, just as he once did.

Self Portrait, Ink on paper, 1972

Art and Deception

As you must know by now, this book is not only about Art Pinajian but this I called *petenaj* on my gmail address, and so too could even our names be confused, as in the small signature on one of his paintings where the i is like a period and reads as: "p.najian."

And it is this missing i that has been the subject of all my work since my first story more than sixty years ago, when I retold an O. Henry tale about an old artist who died painting the last leaf on a wall to save a dying girl as if she were his soul.

I don't know if I have a soul, but I do know I don't know what I am except as a creation, as if my life is itself a work of art that will disappear in the void called sunyata from the root for swollen and thus hollow, like a bubble of foam that will vanish in the sunlight.

"All that we are is the result of what we have thought," says the first line of *The Dhammapada*, translated by Irving Babbitt in my old copy of A New Directions Paperback with a cover photo of shadows on a wall of a Buddhist temple.

And so too was the cause of all my torment, especially in regard to the third verse a few lines further:

"'He abused me, he beat me, he defeated me, he robbed me,'— in those who harbour such thoughts hatred will never cease."

Yes, I myself would cause my cousin Aram to virtually steal Archie's paintings from me, and as always the root my selfhood would lie buried in my old panic that the world would end if I couldn't hold on to it.

My mother had died, but the peace I had hoped for was yet to appear after she was gone, and I was panicked again in that spring in 2006 when I flew east and Aram was to pick me up at Carmela's and drive me to Bellport.

I had arranged with Gwen to include a selection of Archie's paintings in the storage she had rented for Charlie's work in Sacramento, but I didn't know how I was going to deal with the rest in the garage.

I had told Aram I would rent a car to go to Bellport, and I felt grateful when he said he would drive me instead, but why was he so eager to do this when it was such a long drive and all I had asked him for was the key to the bungalow?

I see now that it was because he wanted to make sure I didn't have something up my sleeve.

If I were a film director now I wouldn't really know what to tell the actors playing Aram and me as we rode across the island that morning; they would have to improvise just as I felt I was doing, as if I were acting in the movie of my life and pretending we were the same as when we were kids who loved each other like family.

Yet in all the years I had loved him like an older brother, the truth was that I had rarely seen him as an adult, and there was a part of him that I didn't know at all.

And so as we gossiped and reminisced, I didn't know how to ask him about the living trust my brother had mentioned, and I didn't have the courage to bring it up until we had almost arrived.

And it was really my own deception that would be the root of the anger I would later unleash as if I were betrayed. I cowered as I had always cowered to everyone I loved, always afraid to confront them as if I would lose their love, and even more afraid that I had only imagined our closeness and that I really meant nothing to them at all.

He lied to me, yes, just as he lied to my brother, and he evaded my question about the living trust by saying John was in charge of Armen's property, which had been nothing but a burden to Aram himself, especially since he had so much property of his own.

"I don't need this kind of headache," he said.

But it was not only Aram who deceived me, it was I who deceived him with my devious humility when I asked if John would help me with the cost of shipping and storing the rest of them and promoting them, since I was so anxious about how I could afford this with what little I earned.

We had arrived near Bellport by now, and as we approached the bungalow Aram said yes, he was sure John would help after returning from a business trip.

Then opening the garage I discovered that what I had left in Archie's room had been dumped with the stacks I had covered with plastic, and in the five years Aram and John were supposedly looking after it all, the whole pile had become another mess I would have to sort through again.

I would have to return, I said to Aram, in order to select what would fit in Gwen's storage in Sacramento. So he gave me the key to the bungalow for when my friend Bobby would drive me here on the weekend.

Then after telling him how worried I was about how to ship my selection, he said that he would use the van of the printing company where he was a salesman, and he would ship my selection from its shipping department.

"Thank you, Aram," I said, as if he were doing me a huge favor.

We stopped for lunch on the way back and I thanked him again for paying the check, the subject of the so-called living trust buried in more of our gossip and reminiscence as we drove back across the expressway.

Then inching through the traffic in the Bronx, he got a call on his cell phone from his daughter Lori, and I noticed a relief in his voice when he told her our trip was okay.

But why was she so concerned, I wondered, and now I know why.

My stupidity, I would later realize, had convinced Aram and her that I would not make any trouble; and in the meantime I was still struggling to convince myself that whatever the living trust was about, everything would all work out somehow, since weren't we all family?

Then crossing the George Washington Bridge, I asked him to detour to his home in North Bergen, so I could say hello to Lillian, whom I hadn't seen in the seven years since the hokee-josh for Archie's soul.

And when we arrived in their home in North Bergen, I walked past one of the front rooms whose door was open, and I could see the black plastic trash bags of her hoarding that had filled it to the brim.

And squeezed between them was an old still-life Archie had

given her and Aram for their wedding present that she didn't think was good enough to hang on a wall but held onto to like her hoard of old clothes.

Aram did feel some of Archie's conventional landscapes were pleasing enough to hang in his summer home in Belmar, but he too had called the rest of Archie's paintings "garbage" when he was watching me inspect it in the garage.

He was very tired from the trip, so I asked Lillian to come with us on the drive to Carlstadt, where I would meet Bobby at our friend Sahagian's house, so she could accompany Aram and maybe take the wheel on their drive back to North Bergen.

Gossiping with Lillian before we continued to Carlstadt, I reminisced with her as I did with Aram, but there was a strange look in her eyes I had never seen before, as if I had something up my sleeve.

Looking back now, I did have something up my sleeve, but not what she thought.

I was still deluding myself into thinking we were the family I had imagined since I was boy when she was a sweet young virgin waiting for Aram to return from Korea; but now the green of her eyes that had been so beautiful in my childhood were suddenly hard in a way I had never seen before, as if she were a wary cat that didn't know if I were a friend or foe.

We were acting in a family drama played around the world as far back as King Lear and even further, but unaware of this then, I was still panicked with how to deal with Archie's paintings as if the world would end if I failed.

And so we came to my friend Sahagian's house in Carlstadt where Bobby was visiting, and since Aram knew Sahag and Bobby from the old days in our Armenian circle, we chatted in the yard until Aram and Lillian were to leave, and then Aram promised me again he would ship my selection to Gwen as soon as he could.

Then at Carmela's that night, I couldn't fall asleep worrying about John helping me with the cost of storing the rest of the paintings and promoting them, and I stayed awake until morning when I could call Lillian and ask her for John's phone number.

"What do you want it for?" she said when I called, and there was a strange hardness in her voice.

And when I told her about storing and promoting the paintings she said:

"You know, Peter, if you're thinking about contesting the will, there's nothing you can do about it."

"What are you talking about?" I said, suddenly shocked.

And she went on and on, as if I had something up my sleeve.

"I don't know what you're talking about," I said.

"Oh, come on," she said, "don't play naïve with me."

And she hung up.

"Aram," I said, calling him immediately after she hung up. "What was Lillian talking about?"

"What did you call her for?" he said angrily, and it was the first time in all the years I had known him that he was ever angry with me.

"I told you I would talk with John," he said. "Now you've opened up a can of worms and I'll never hear the end of it."

What can of worms? What was he so angry about?

Carmela was at her computer on the other side of the room, and when I put the phone down, she said:

"What was that all about?"

And with my nerves stretched to their breaking point, not only from the lack of sleep, but my life of panic as if my world was coming to an end, I suddenly started crying as I tried to tell her how my cousins were like my family, and my tears pressed the anger button of her own family history:

"Pete," she said, "that family crap is all bullshit; there is no family; your friends are your family; there's no one else."

"Orion", Ink on paper, 1984

Art and Hoarding

Aram's marriage was the can of worms that my call to Lillian had opened. He had never really wanted Armen's property. He had plenty of property of his own, and greed was not the root of his character.

He had his own kind of stinginess and money lust, yet it was not to hoard but to act like a big shot and join the country club where he would play golf with the rich and famous.

He was also a dreamer, and driving alone in the long hours of his life as a salesman, he would invent stories like those he read in his gluttony for books. And so he really did want to imagine Armen left her home to his grandkids whom she had never seen, and sincerely fond of her himself he too had tried to talk her into getting a reverse mortgage to spend her property away.

He was not, as my brother had said, a bad person, and what he would do to me was because I didn't mean as much to him as I thought, and he really was as my brother said, "pussy-whipped."

He loved his wife and he was devoted to his family, and on our trip to Bellport he did try in his round about way to explain not welcoming me to stay in his home.

He had been trying for years to cure Lillian of her hoarding, but after John and Lori were gone it grew beyond his control, and now like her trash bags Armen's property had become a burden to him when he had to drive back and forth to Bellport in order to deal with it.

"I didn't need this kind of headache," he had said when drove me there, and it would be the last time I would see him for the rest of our lives.

Lillian herself was not a bad person in the addiction of her sickness, and somewhere inside me knew this even when I cried in Carmela's apartment.

She grew up poor after her father died when she was only a kid and her older brother was mentally ill and her mother could barely pay the rent, and she would take care of them for the rest of their lives.

Now she would work just as hard to help her daughter and her four grandkids, and she would do anything to keep them from ever being in want.

She didn't do anything wrong to me in grabbing Armen's home; I was the one who was wrong in imagining I was family to her.

* * *

Yet all I could think about when I rode with Bobby to Bellport was how to make my selection of Archie's paintings: Archie's paintings, Archie's paintings, always Archie's paintings, as if they had become my own kind of hoarding.

And so once again I rushed in a panic to select what I could to ship to Gwen, just as I had panicked after Archie died; but now I had only an afternoon before Bobby had to return to his new home in Westchester, and I struggled to make my selection while Bobby lunched in the little town and then napped in his car.

I still didn't know what I would do with the rest of the work after the house was sold, but all I could do now was to have my selection shipped to Gwen and deal with the rest later.

Then after stacking my selection in the bungalow with the dimensions Aram had said would fit in his company's van, I wrote a note to him with Gwen's address.

I had included with my selection a small oil portrait Charlie had painted of Armen when he was a student at Pratt and she was only eighteen, which she had hung in her bedroom till the day she died, and I ask Aram to make sure Gwen would see it when she unpacked the shipment.

Then locking the front door and slipping the key under the mat by the back door, I left with Bobby for his new home in Westchester where I would spend the night before flying back to Berkeley.

This was in April of 2006.

A letter from the Suffolk County Courthouse came to Charlie and me a few weeks later, including a copy of the will in case we wanted to contest it.

And when I saw the date of Armen's signature in 2001, my rage burst in flames, and I wrote to Aram in my fury.

"How could you lie to Tom and me?" I wrote. "How could you tell us all that crap about a living trust?"

And I wrote on and on describing his deception, and I mailed copies of my letter to Bobby and Sahagian to expose his perfidy to our Armenian circle, as if making it public would be my revenge.

And it was my vengeance that would lead to more of my pain, as vengeance always does.

"For never does hatred cease by hatred," the Dhammapada would say. "This is an eternal law."

"Why did you have to broadcast it?" Aram said when I called him.

But all I wanted to know was when he was going to ship my selection to Gwen.

He wouldn't be able to get to it, he said, until after he recovered from his knee surgery.

And so I waited another month, and this time he said he was having trouble selling the bungalow and would get back to me.

And so the months passed while he lied to me each time I called to ask when he was going to ship my selection to Gwen.

But he never would of course, and his delay was his own revenge at my exposing him, which would lead to the destiny of Archie's paintings that I would never see again.

* * *

Then one day in the middle of March of the following year, I got a note in the mail from my friend Peter Nagourney in Ann Arbor, who had enclosed a page from the Metro Section of the New York Times.

It was about an Armenian painter in Long Island, by a reporter, Cory Kilgannon, who wrote:

"Closing on a House, and a Life's Story, Told in Art."

"Pete," Nagourney said in his note, "do you know this guy Pinajian?"

A businessman named Larry Joseph had bought the bungalow "as is for $300,000," and Joseph's partner, Thomas Schultz, would renovate and resell it for a profit.

But when Shultz inspected the property he found what I had left behind in the garage.

"A cousin of the Pinajians," wrote Kilgannon, " said his family already owned plenty of the paintings and felt that Mr. Joseph and Mr. Schultz 'had a better chance' of getting this unappreciated artist some recognition."

And it was the phrase "as is" that inflamed my rage again, since it meant that the paintings could have been dumped had Thomas Schultz not recognized their value.

"How could you do that, Aram?" I said to him when I called.

But instead of answering, he twisted my anger into his own, as if I had betrayed him by "shooting my mouth off to everyone."

"What did you do with my selection?" I said.

"I got it," he said, and he hung up.

And it would not be until months later when I met Thomas Schultz that he would tell me he didn't go into the bungalow but only the garage when he inspected the property.

Shultz lived near Bellport, and he had told his partner Larry Joseph, who had moved to Beverly Hills, about an old cottage for sale, and Joseph told him to arrange the sale so they could "flip it," as they had done with a previous venture.

When Shultz spoke with John and Lillian about the work in the garage:

"They said it was worthless and I could dump it; but I said, 'Oh, no, it may be very valuable.'"

I asked Shultz if he had seen my selection in the bungalow, and he said no, there was nothing there.

So learning the value of my selection, Aram and Lillian must have returned with the printing company's van before the sale was finalized, and they took my selection back to Jersey where it would be locked in storage like Lillian's hoard of plastic bags in her home.

I called Aram to reach Larry Joseph, but he wouldn't tell me how, so I called the Times to find Kilgannon, who gave me Joseph's number in Beverly Hills.

Then Joseph said he wanted to meet me. He was originally

from Manhattan, and his mother, who still lived there, would be visiting his new home in Beverly Hills.

Wanting to show his mother the rest of California, he would drive up to the Bay Area and see me on the way.

In the meantime I had called an old high school friend, Renato Biribin, who was now a lawyer in Newark, and I asked him to help me get my selection back from Aram and Lillian.

I told Renato our mutual friends Bobby and Sahag had witnessed Aram promise to ship my selection to Gwen, and I also had a letter from Armen saying I could get whatever I wanted from Aram, so Renato wrote Aram a letter in legalese to please return them, as if threatening a lawsuit.

Thinking I could get my selection back with Renato's help, I intended to partner with Joseph in whatever promotion he might plan, and so I gave him a copy of my biography that included the letters I had edited, plus some Xerox copies of my collection of war drawings and comics.

But no sooner had I done this, when Renato returned my call and said that he never got a reply from Aram's lawyer, and since I had no document of a promise, a judge would dismiss my case as frivolous.

"Give it up, Pete," Renato said. "There's nothing you can do."

And so I rushed an email to Joseph telling him to send me back my manuscript and the copies of the drawings and comics, but it was too late, he had already mailed them to a promoter back east.

Enamel on paper, 1994

Art and Promotion

L*arry Joseph* was an honest businessman, and though I was upset when he didn't ask permission to send my work to a promoter, I did lead him to think I cared only about what he called Archie's "legacy," which was why I had worked so hard in editing the letters and writing my biography.

He had even encouraged me to publish it on line and said he would help with his connections.

A friendly and straightforward man, he invited me to dinner with his mother at the affordable part of Berkeley's famous culinary attraction, Chez Panisse, and we reminisced about our ethnic roots back east, where he had grown up in an Assyrian community like my Armenian one.

He was very bright and energetic (see Wikipedia), and in exchange for my giving him a copy of my novel, *Daughters of Memory*, he sent me his recent book, *Apocalypse 2012*, in which I learned he was an accomplished writer with a strong voice.

I liked him and I had thought I could work with him before Renato told me to let go of getting my selection back. His ex-wife was an ambitious actress who had moved to L.A. to further her career, and following her there to be with his young daughters to whom he was devoted, he was now saddled with a huge alimony to pay each month, but he had an optimistic and adventurous nature and he was not afraid to take chances.

He didn't, however, know anything about art, and banking on Shultz' enthusiasm for Archie's paintings, he asked me tell him sincerely what I thought of them.

"Are they really good?" he asked me innocently.

I had told him about my selection, and worried that his leftovers were not as good, he was relieved when I assured him I had chosen only what would fit in Aram's company van and there was more than plenty of the same in the garage.

Then by chance about a month later, Thomas Shultz and his wife Mary came with their baby Lila on vacation to San Francisco where Mary had a close friend, and when they came to Berkeley I gave them a tour of Telegraph Avenue, where we had lunch in a "gourmet" sandwich shop before he interviewed me in my cottage with his video camera.

They were a bright-faced and attractive couple who had grown up near Bellport, where Thomas had always wanted to live when he was a kid, and Mary had just started her practice as a psychotherapist.

Thomas was a go-getter with boundless enthusiasm for every one of his projects, but none ever panned out as he dreamed, and I imagined Mary was now helping to pay the bills while he embarked on his new venture.

Larry had met Thomas in one of those projects that was a little café in Bellport, and they became friends while flipping an old cottage Thomas had renovated before he found Armen's.

He had always loved art though he didn't know much about it, and he was very excited when he saw what was in the garage; then finding Archie's Bronze star in the attic, he grew even more excited by his nostalgia for World War II as if he had discovered a forgotten hero.

So of course he was more than excited when I showed him the war drawings and the comics, and he wanted me to join what he called his "team" of his new "Pinajian Project."

Larry would pay me nothing while investing so much in it, but Thomas was sure I would be compensated when I would sell what I had in my personal collection after the big bucks started rolling in.

Back in Bellport Thomas had a friend whose sister was married to an art scholar, William Homer (see Wikipedia), who agreed to look at the images Thomas had sent him, and Homer then recommended a promoter, Peter Hastings Falk,(see Wikipedia.)

By synchronicity, Falk had already tacked on his corkboard the same article by Corey Kilgannon that my friend Nagourney had sent to me, and Falk had already intended to contact Larry.

Kilgannon was a friend of a friend of Thomas, which was how the article in the N.Y. Times came to be written.

Then after Larry sent Falk my manuscript with the copies of the war drawings and comics, I got a call from Falk, and we got off on the wrong foot from the moment I tried to tell him about how Aram virtually stole my selection.

"I don't want to hear about your family's dirty laundry," he said.

And we would never get along from that moment on.

All he wanted, he said, was my collection of Archie's letters and the war drawings and comics. And when I refused, he threatened that I would never be able to publish them without Larry who owned their copyright as owner of the estate.

So cowering to his threat and reminding myself that all I really cared about was Archie anyway, I agreed to be part of the book he was putting together that he would call his "monograph."

And when he called himself a "historian," I asked if he were getting paid for his work, and he said:

"I'm not doing this for fun."

In fact, I would later learn his deal with Larry was a percentage of the take. He did have a passion for art history, but from what I gathered his personal taste did not include Archie's kind of work, and I didn't think he really understood it.

But he respected Homer's view of it, and he was sure he could market it by exploiting Archie's background as a comic book pioneer who had won a Bronze Star and as a contemporary of the abstract expressionists.

He was a hard worker, and in using my biography he added his own research and called his version of my manuscript his "biographical essay" in his promotional book, which I had to accept for Archie's sake, though I felt it was a plagiarism of my work, especially my editing of the letters.

He did however include some excerpts from a short memoir he asked me to write, but he said nothing about me in his acknowledgements except:

"Peter Najarian supplied a series of letters…and excerpts from his essay are from his as-yet unpublished memoir."

In the meantime the introduction to his book was a very brief chapter by Homer whose comments upset me deeply:

"Pinajian makes an interesting psychological case study. There were two sides to his personality—one embodying a lyrical, romantic view of nature, and the other exposing the darker side of male fantasies... a significant proportion of his work [sic his doodles and sketches] concerned itself with erotica, primarily female. Erotic nudes seem to be an obsession...."

But I would ignore this, since Homer saw only what Schultz had shown him and was ignorant of Archie's playful take on the nude that came from a background in comics and the Penthouse magazines he used in lieu of models, especially under the influence of Henry Miller around the time Archie was writing The Model and The Mountain, in which he was imitating Miller's candor and openness.

Homer had also ignored Archie's tender female figures, especially the truly beautiful ones like those in my selection that the Aram was hoarding, a few of which are in the slides I still have, where the delicacy of their light is like Renoir's.

It was however Falk's use of Homer's distorted view that would really upset me so deeply in the months to come. And Larry would add to this distortion in his concluding memoir chapter:

"....After poking through the piles," Larry wrote, "all I could think was that the stuff was brilliant, but I had to be wrong. Treasure troves don't just drop from the sky into the laps of guys like me.

"Then Mary [Thomas' wife], a psychologist, said something reassuring. She was of the opinion that the artist, though powerfully talented and driven, was likely given to psychotic episodes and may well have suffered from a bipolar disorder. A talented loonie with overwhelming needs popping up from the middle of nowhere....

"Mary observed that Pinajian's females are too often depicted in dark settings [sic], recumbent at unnatural angles and with breasts that defy gravity.... Her conclusions as a psychologist are that Pinajian had a powerful attraction to women but had no ability to establish relationships with them...."

But I dismissed the above as I did Homer's remarks, since I was grateful for Archie's sake for how much Larry had invested in his Pinajian Project, which according to Thomas "was over $250, 000," which included the cost of Falk's promotional book, called "Pinajian: Master of Abstraction Discovered."

Except for its errors and distortions, it did give a decent view of Archie's development, though it was geared to his comics and his early derivative work and not that of his maturity, which was more important, especially to Archie.

And so I was grateful for its centerpiece, The Amazing Adventures of Arthur Pinajian, by Richard J. Boyle [see Google], which was a brief history of comics and Archie's part in it.

Unfortunately it too had errors I could have corrected had I been consulted, such as Archie studying in the League in "1936" instead of a decade later and "using photography as an aide memoire," as in the photograph of Archie on the floor, when posing for Charlie in a photographer's studio for one of Charlie's illustration jobs.

But unlike Homer, Boyle did recognize what was behind Archie's female figures:

"While Pinajian soon became a painter immersed in Abstract Expressionism, a parallel body of his figurative work shows that the comic book mode was one that he never gave up entirely. His extensive body of erotica…is informed by a combination of his comic book art, illustration, and the works of both old and modern masters… where the figures very much resemble those of the Matisse painting, The Joy of Life.

"Thus, Pinajian's erotica were not the result of a clandestine pursuit. This large part of the collection does not represent an excursus to his main collection of abstract works but an important part of his life.

"Any Freudian interpretations not withstanding, these erotic works seemed to reflect his urge to return to comics and illustration. Some of the faces he drew are reminiscent of Japanese anime from the early 1960's, while other are appropriated from Playboy, and later from Victoria's Secret catalogues. Some seem even destined for a comic book or graphic novel, while others are executed in a stylized and simplified approach that combines book composition with the art of Henri Matisse....

"After all, he had made money at it in the past, and this prospect may have been part of his sporadic return to it."

Thank you, Richard Boyle.

I would, for Archie's sake, even thank Falk, who was both a skilled researcher and promoter and worked hard to make his book as financially successful as he could.

And so I tried to let go of being upset by Falk claiming my own work as his own. His research and the biographical part of his book would have been a skeleton without all that I had supplied, but I had to remind myself that all my own work had been for Archie's sake, and it was selfish of me to complain that I received nothing for it.

Everything I did was for Archie's sake, always for Archie's sake, but now Archie was dead and gone, and I didn't want anything more to do with Falk's book or anything else involving the paintings that I would never see again.

And yet I later got deeply upset again by how Falk would then develop his promotion around what he introduced in the preface to his book:

"The Vonnegut Coincidence: In 1987, Kurt Vonnegut published Bluebeard: The Autobiography of Rabo Karabekian (1916-1988), a novel about an eccentric painter whose life bears an astonishing resemblance to Arthur Pinajian....

"Vonnegut's artist defined himself as a 'Fiasco in which a person causes total destruction of [his] own work and reputation through stupidity, carelessness or both.'

"Pinajian left instructions for his collection to be discarded in the town dump. Neither artist's painting would have been shown publicly but for outside intervention—in Bluebeard's case a nosy friend; and in Pinajian's case, some nosy art historians, namely us."

And so all my flying back and forth to save Archie's work and get it shown, all my labor in editing his letters and writing his biography,

all my troubles with Armen and Aram and all my heartache and torment, would all now be buried in the garbage Falk would cite in his
promotion in the years ahead.

"What are you going to do with all these paintings?" I had said
to Archie that day we stood in the garage looking at the hole in the
little canvas where a bird had woven her nest, and he had said, "I'm
leaving them all to you."

I loved him like a father, and like I imagined my father, he was
one of the most sane human beings I had ever known, who never
hurt anyone and never complained and wanted only to do keep
drawing lines like the child who once scribbled on his mother's
kitchen table, a popular and attractive and humorous man whom
everyone liked and who was outgoing and socially responsible and
whose isolation in his later years was the result only of his poverty
and the kind of society he lived in.

And now he was being turned into an eccentric hermit with a
bi-polar dark side.

But why did I care anymore? What was it to me?

Why was I so upset when Falk insisted on calling him Arthur
after I complained that he wanted to be known as Art, which was
how he signed his work. No, Falk had said, echoing Armen whom
Archie would call "The Duchess," it was not "respectable" enough,
as if it were like Art Carney, the comedian.

And why was I getting even more upset by reading that Archie
was supposed to have "left instructions for his work to be discarded
in the town dump?"

So what? Who cared? What difference did it make?

No, as always when pointing to others with blame, three of the
fingers in my fist were pointing to myself.

It was I myself who had been the cause of my torment when
Thomas interviewed me and I mentioned Armen said Archie told
her to throw his work in the garbage.

And Thomas would give his video tape to a filmmaker, Donald
Prudem, who would in his You Tube cut out the part where I said
Archie had made his remark only in a moment of annoyance when she
had nagged him, just as she was nagging me when she quoted him.

And Falk would use the edited version as the basis for the comparison to Bluebeard and the rescue by historians.

No, my torment was not Falk's fault; he was just doing his job the only way he knew, which was to sell as many paintings as he could by inventing a story in which of course he had to leave out my "dirty laundry."

It was what promoters had done since paintings came out of the caves where they were not to be seen but made with the same magic as a child's scribble of snakes on a table top.

What was promotion itself but a form of civilization that was built on getting and spending, while the blood of an artist turned to dust and his work became a myth that would feed historians and salesmen for generations to come.

Yes, my torment was not for Archie's sake and no one's fault but my own, I was my own discontent.

Once upon a time I had a cousin Archie whom I loved as if he were a father, and like I once stopped lighting candles after my father died, I would never do anything for Archie's sake again.

And so the wheels of the Pinajian Project began to roll, and I wanted nothing to do with them. In fact, any news of them just reminded me of my pain.

Acrylic on paper, April 1985

Art and The Bible

F*ollowing the self-publication* of his book, Falk summarized it in the American Art Review, Vol. XXII, No. 4, 2010, a magazine of "representational art in regional museums."

He then succeeded in hanging an exhibit he called "Arthur Pinajian, Master of Abstraction Discovered," at the Woodstock Artists Association Museum, from July to October, 2010.

I didn't fly back for it of course, or for the next exhibit at the Armenian Library and Museum of America in Watertown, MA, from November to March 2011.

Or the one in St. Leon Armenian Cathedral-Zorayan Museum in Burbank, CA, from May to June 2011.

Expert at his profession, Falk targeted the wealthy Armenians in the Boston and Los Angeles areas, but his "throw it in the garbage" and "Bluebeard" routine continued to anger me.

In fact his distortion of Archie's character and his exploitation of my manuscript made me so angry, I started re-writing these chapters, which are actually my second re-write. The first was after Aram's betrayal when Larry sent my original biography to Falk.

So I've actually been working on this story since Archie died sixteen years ago, when I began to edit his letters and wrote about him to promote his work.

Then ironically it was Falk himself who was promoting it, though at the expense of making Archie into an eccentric hermit who wanted his work thrown to the garbage, which I myself stupidly caused by shooting my mouth off when I let Schultz tape me in his interview.

They were of course just trying to make a buck, which has always been the other face of art, at least in the age of galleries.

And though the Pinajian project hasn't made it into the big New York galleries, it reached the Armenians who have been as good as Jews at making more than a buck, and they came through in getting Larry back his $250, 000, plus so much more.

* * *

The Pinajian promotion hit the market just after the big crash in 2008, but paintings could still be a good investment, and as George Orwell once wrote, quoting an old canard, "It would take four Jews" to outsmart an Armenian in any business deal, so Falk was smart to appeal to such a mercantile people.

The Armenians were originally a mountain people and not traders like the sea-faring Phoenicians, but they had moved into the valleys and plains, and they became Christians around the time the Romans converted, which became a good move in the golden age of Justinian.

And though becoming Christian turned lethal after Islam took over, they were fierce in holding onto their identity in which their Bible would be their glue, just as the Hebrew Bible was for the Jews who would share with Armenians their own history of genocide.

In fact it was in an Armenian Bible that my grandfather had written the names of his children, which had come down to my cousin Manooshag after the massacre.

I couldn't read these names, nor could Little Aram who would virtually steal that Bible from me, since neither of us knew the Armenian script in which they had been written or the Armenian translation of the Bible itself, but we both treasured what it stood for, which was our idea of a family.

The Armenian alphabet was invented by a genius monk in the age of Armenia's great medieval monasteries, and though I never learned it like many of my Jewish friends barely learned the Hebrew alphabet, the curls of its lines were like threads to somewhere deep inside me I didn't want to let go.

I wanted that Bible, I said to Little Aram over the phone when I asked for Archie's paintings back. His mother Manooshag had verbally willed it to me because I was the last Najarian, and he heard her say this himself.

My father's name was written in the flyleaf, I said, and I wanted it as if it were my father himself. It wasn't even Manooshag's, I said, or even my grandfather's. According to my mother, the Bible had belonged to my grandfather's first wife.

Family was everything to my orphan mother, and adopting

my father's family, she would with her love of stories recite the Najarian saga as if it were her own Genesis.

My grandfather's first wife, she would say, was a devout young woman from Kharpet who had died young when her two boys, Boghos and Garabed, were still toddlers. [See them in the photo in Chapter One.]

And when Garabed married the sister of the Semerjians, my grandfather gave the Bible to them for their wedding.

Who knows why it was not to his oldest son, Boghos, who would become Manooshag's father? Maybe because Garabed married first?

In any case, it must have been with Garabed's widow after he and Boghos were executed as leaders of an underground resistance group.

Her Moslem neighbor had saved her from the massacre and she didn't want to leave their children when her sister-in-law, Boghos' wife and Manooshag's mother, was escaping to Alexandria.

And so she must have given the Bible to Manooshag's mother, which was how Manooshag would inherit it. Then holding it in trust, Manooshag wanted to pass it to me in trust as well.

And now I wanted it, I said to her son, Little Aram, who had betrayed me.

No, he said, I had no children and he was keeping it for his grandkids, and he hung up.

His daughter Lori had married an Irishman whose half-Irish kids wouldn't know the Najarian name from Adam or the unreadable book in a strange alphabet.

It was true I had no children, but I could leave it to any of several Armenian libraries or cultural museums.

Yes, my attachment was part of what Blake would call a "Selfhood," but this selfhood was also entwined with art like a sinew to a bone, and my life was in art as much as Archie's.

A sadhu or a nun would let go of a family name to find a realm beyond the self, but a name was language itself, and language was my own way to the all-embracing AUM of the great and nameless Void.

And even the name Najarian, from the Akkadian *najar* for carpenter, might lead to that embrace like mortise and tenon in the
great household of my longing.

There were few last names among ordinary Turkish-Armenians
in the Nineteenth Century, and my grandfather, who was
Manooshag's and Archie's and Charlie's grandfather, was named
Najar-yan because he was a carpenter, and I was their cousin because I was a Najar-yan too.

And so I wanted that Bible with my father's name in it, I didn't
want it to go to Little Aram's grandkids whose last names were Irish
and whose own grandfather had betrayed me.

But there was no way I could get it unless I embraced him and
forgave him, and even then he wouldn't give it back.

To tell the truth, it was not the Bible I wanted to hold onto,
but my longing for a family and my own need to write my own
bible, so to speak, the book of my life so engraved with my loneliness like a Job's and my voice in a wilderness.

* * *

Yes, my selfhood was a desolation of abomination always
searching for a home, since that very day I first left my mother's
kitchen while she was caring for my father after his stroke.

It must have been in the following year in the spring of 1945,
because I remember walking around the corner and seeing the
Jewish kids in their new Yeshiva that had been the public school
where my brother had gone before it was sold.

I remember this because I had yet to start kindergarten, which
wouldn't begin until the fall, and the sun was shining and the
Jewish kids were playing in the schoolyard on the other side of the
iron fence looking so happy and alive.

I too felt a kind of happiness so full of life myself, and I had no
memory of my father's stroke or my mother's unhappiness.

All I would remember was how sunny and alive the Jewish
children seemed, as if they were a vision of an Eden on the other
side of the fence where I wanted to join them.

And yet my memory went back even before then, because I

would remember a photographer's studio where the photographer told me to hold a wooden rifle that I wanted to keep, and in the photograph I wore a soldier's uniform like Charlie and Archie who were in the war then.

I always thought it was my mother who told me I couldn't keep the rifle, but no, she said a lifetime later, it was my father who had taken me to the photographer.

Why then couldn't I remember him when I could remember the rifle so vividly?

All I would remember were his lips twisted by the stroke and the slur of his voice that only my mother could understand, nor could I remember the sudden thunderbolt of the stroke itself when my mother was suddenly gone in her trips to the hospital.

Yet I could remember the photographer's studio and how much I wanted that wooden rifle that must have been before the stroke, if it really was my father who had taken me there.

Then like a movie where the shock and the horror were cut away, my next memory would be of that happy morning when my mother said I could go outside by myself, and I walked around the corner and saw the Jewish kids in their new Yeshiva, as if the nightmare of the war had dissolved into a sunny pastoral.

And it must have been soon after that the war ended, because I would remember everyone shouting and blowing horns when the air was filled with confetti like a vision of joy and fulfillment.

And the next memory would be of the excitement of going to kindergarten in Hudson Grammar School so far away on the other side of town.

No, I can't remember any unhappiness then, I remember only being a happy child, and I have no memory of any pain or misery.

And yet one day a lifetime later, I happened to be chatting with Donald Negrini, the older brother of my kindergarten friend, Dennis, and Donald reminisced about my crying outside Hudson School because my brother didn't come to take me home, and Donald had to walk me all the way home to the other side of town.

Yet I can't remember any of this.

I remember later walking to kindergarten myself, so I must

have learned how to weave through those eleven blocks from the trolley tracks to the cliffs, yet I can't remember any unhappiness, but only the adventure of seeing the seagulls fly above the reservoir each morning.

No, the darker memories wouldn't surface until later, like the egg of a moth in an apple blossom that would hatch in the seed and continue feeding until the core of the apple was black and bitter.

So that in a recent trip to Los Angeles just a few months ago, when I suddenly panicked at being lost on the freeways, I felt like a child who had lost his way home and I would die if I didn't find it.

Why did I panic at being lost, my friend Bob Maniquis said, "Why not accept it as an adventure?"

And it was true that in my youth I had adventured around the world where it was impossible to be lost because I was always on the road.

But I had grown old and weary and alone.

What was the difference between "weary" and "tired," Bob's daughter Sarah had asked, and he said the body feels tired but weary is what the soul feels.

And so I've come to the end of these chapters and what happens to art after an artist grows old and dies.

If you remember, I started them at a garbage dump in Tenafly with a painting by a George Chapman that may have been stolen by one of the moving men after Charlie mentioned how valuable it was.

But what are all these chapters really about, all these lines about art and a betrayal? What is the real story?

What is the Bible really about, all those stories about families and betrayals and what happened after Jews became Christians and Rembrandt and Blake transformed them into visions?

My little mind is too small to make sense of it all, and who will read my book but a few friends before it too is buried in a dump?

* * *

And so I end with a printmaking workshop at a local community college where it was fun at first learning how to engrave a plate like my heroes Rembrandt and Blake had done, until I had no need of extra copies or any patience for the chemistry and precision.

I did enjoy the magic of the stone in lithography, but I soon gave it up as well, having again no need of copies or any patience for the labor of printing them.

And so I turned to monotypes like my sketch of young Yana who was working on her litho stone near my table.

She was born in southern China and would soon enroll in an art college where she would learn fashion design.

Yet in my sketch she was not Yana anymore, she was the eternal art student who had become my soul: the girl who would embrace me in the circle of Eden like the sunlight on those Jewish kids in the new Yeshiva on the other side of the iron fence.

She was the daughter and wife I never had, the home and family of my longing.

But where was the father I never became?

He was not Archie; no, Archie was never a father but only used me as his Sancho Panza. I had to be my own father and make him whole again. Hephaestus too was a cripple, but he wove into his lines the Goddess of Lust and the God of Massacre until he would let them go.

And the litho stone on which my soul was drawing was the same limestone as in the great cave of my grandparents who painted the slaughtered bison with the charcoal of the fire that was the gift of Prometheus.

And in that stone were drawings upon drawings buried under the grinding of the levigator like Yana's drawing would be ground away by the next art student.

She was actually drawing on all the drawings of the previous centuries, just as the cave people drew bison and horses on all the other bison and horses of the previous millennia.

I am trying, you see, to put it all together, like Rembrandt and Blake drawing upon the genius of the past.

"Love Genius," Blake said, "It is the face of God."

If you don't grind the stone clean, the buried drawings will surface like memories you don't want to remember.

You must grind it and wash it until the stone is as smooth as soap, and then you can draw a fresh image that you can print before the next artist rubs it away.

In a monotype, however, it is the leftover print called the "ghost" that you really want to keep, like a memory of a drawing on the wall by my bed in my childhood.

I am, you see, talking to myself now, and you have become my self, or maybe my soul.

I used you to help me continue writing my chapters because it was so hard to write to the great garbage dump, but you were so far away and I was really writing to myself like a child playing with her dolls.

"Yana," monotype and ghost, by Pete, 2013

* * *

And so I end with the memory of when I first started drawing with a little pencil on the wall by my bed in that little bedroom I shared with my older brother in the railroad apartment on Bergenline Avenue in West Hoboken.

It must have been when I started kindergarten and saw in the little neighborhood movie house a cowboy movie with Gene Autry, or was it the Durango Kid?

And I drew his horse in between the pits and cracks of the painted plaster of the wall by my bed.

I had no talent for drawing like my brother who could draw with either hand, but who cared, I just wanted to draw how much I loved that horse.

It was not any horse, you see, it was not even Gene Autry's or the Durango Kid's, it was the horse in the cave of our forgotten dreams, and the plaster with its pits and cracks was the limestone buried between the stalagmites and stalactites.

I was, you see, not only me or my ancestors, but my cousins Charlie and Archie who kept drawing until their very end, which is what this book is really about and not what happens to art after an artist dies or the wound of a betrayal or the venality of the marketplace.

It is about an eternal child drawing on a plaster wall that a great mother would wipe away, not really for the great garbage dump of the void, but only so more lines could snake into millennia after millennia.

Bill Belli's Mustang by Pete, oil on paper, 2002 [color altered by reproduction]

Yes, it is what all stories and drawings are really about, not
something to be sold or preserved or locked in a vault, but why
that primeval artist went so deep into that cave like a child who
loved a horse.

And so I return to my cousin Archie, as if my story were a movie
where the camera zooms from the caves of art to a boy sitting in a
ferry to his job as a clerk in a carpet factory in lower Manhattan.

He once told me he learned anatomy from a book on his ferry
ride to work, and so let us look at him now on the great river of art
as the ferry sails to the other shore:

Behind him, in the little town of West New York on the cliff
above the river, his mother is dying of intestinal cancer, and his
father and his uncle have become jobless by the great Depression,
and his clerk's pay is all that keeps them from the wolf at the door.

He will tally numbers from morning to evening ten hours a
day, but the ferry is slow and calm as he opens to the first chapter
of his anatomy book.

"It is between me and myself that I work now," he will write a
lifetime later.

"My work is a reflection of what I want my life to be.

"To understand the totality of art is to arrive at its creation.

*"If you are conscious of Totality, time will coalesce everything
into one.*

Look at him now as if in a movie of this book while he follows
how each sinew leads into another.

They are of course not just the human body, but the sinews of all
life that bind not only our muscles to our bones but why Leonardo
would study them and draw the Vitruvian Man with his arms reach-
ing to the infinite that Blake would copy in *The Glad Day*.

And so will my Archie study them and draw his series, "That
Ol' Gang O' Mine," like the great gang of art that will be his totality and my totality, while the ferry crosses to the other shore in the
wake of history where all our memories will bubble and disappear
in the white foam.

From Pete's collection of acrylic or enamel on paper,
1993-1999

Additional slides from the selection, oil on canvas

Afterword

Five *years passed* after Archie's paintings hit the marketplace in 2010, and in that same year my book, *The Artist and His Mother,* was published by The Press at California State University, Fresno.

I offered the Press this book, and after they sat on it for three years before declining, I turned to another small press that also sat on it for another year until I finally decided to publish it myself.

And so I found Mark Weiman's Regent Press that happened to be just up the street, which reminded me of how I once published *Daughters of Memory* with my friend Mike Helm and his *City Miner Books* here in Berkeley as well.

My friend Bobby would help me by ordering a hundred copies, and other friends also pledged to buy copies, and so Mark and I began sitting at his computer placing into the text my photos and collection of Archie's works, including those on 11 by 14 paper, which he would do each day along with the larger canvasses in oil that were taken from me.

Then a few days ago, in the late evening before Mark would send the completed file to the printer in Tennessee, I got an email from Australia:

"Hi Pete, Sarah Allely here, I'm with Australian Public broadcaster SBS TV. I have been speaking with Thomas Schultz and Lawrence Joseph about Arthur Pinajian's work. It would be great to get your perspective. The time difference between Berkeley and Sydney is awkward, so it would be great if you could get back to me tonight please. If you flick me your number, I'll call you. Otherwise, let's make a time to speak tomorrow afternoon please? Thanks, Sarah"

I summarized my "perspective" in my reply, but I wouldn't be home the following day until late in the evening, and after a hectic email exchange in which I couldn't fit into the rush of her schedule my interview was canceled. She was wrapping up her broadcast that night, she said, and it would be aired on a program called

"Insight" on the subject of "Windfalls" the following week on May 19. When I Googled Insight and Windfalls I found:

"Ever imagine what life would be like if you suddenly hit the jackpot? From winning a game show or the lotto, receiving an inheritance to finding and flipping a valuable antique, Insight hears from people who have found instant wealth. Did they squander their riches or set themselves up for life? Guests will talk about how their life-changing windfall impacted on their identity and relationships. How does an increased fortune change the winners and the behaviour of those around them."

Thomas Schultz had been interviewed on the same subject in an episode of ABC's Dateline about two years ago. He made enough money, he said, to send his three kids to college.

It is now May 15, 2015, and Mark will add this afterword to the file before emailing it to the printer in Tennessee.

2nd Street, Berkeley, oil on paperboard, by Pete, 2014

OTHER TITLES BY REGENT PRESS

Misadventures of a Scientists Wife
[about Noble Prize winner Charles Townes]
by Frances Townes

The Viet Arcane
by Jack Hirschman

The Ecology of Consciousness Series (7 vols.)
by Ralph Metzner

A Terrible Beauty
The Wilderness of American Literature
by Jonah Raskin

The Storied Ice
Exploration, Discovery, and Adventure
in Antarctica's Peninsula Region
by Joan N. Boothe

Charles Darwin in Cyberspace
by Claire Burch

Traditional Themes in Japanese Art
by Charles R. Temple

Weapon: Mouth
by Stoney Burke

Gold Fever / San Francisco - 1851
by Ken Salter

Sexual Accusation and Social Turmoil
by Jules Masserman, MD

The San Francisco Oracle Facsimile Edition
The Psychedelic Newspaper of the Haight Ashbury
by Alan Cohen, ed.

Goddesses, Goddesses
by Janine Canan

VIVO [Voice-In / Voice Out]
The Coming Age of Talking Computers
by William Crossman

Visions of Frisco
Illustrated by Satty

Highway House
by Bob Pritikin

Madness at the Gates of The City
The Myth of American Innocence
by Barry Spector

Dr. Toy's Smart Play / Smart Toys
How to Select and Use the Best Toys and Games
by Stevanne Auerbach ("Dr. Toy)

September Snow
by Robert Balmanno

An Eye for an Eye Makes the Whole World Blind / Poets on 9/11
by Alan Cohen and Clive Matson, eds.

Crimes & Offenses
by Judy Koretsky

Urban Impressions
Photography by Marianne Robinson

CPSIA information can be obtained at www.ICGtesting.com
Printed in the USA
BVOW10s1032080715

407652BV00006B/48/P

9 781587 903212